Farm to Fable

Robert Grillo

Foreword by Carol J. Adams

 Vegan Pul

GW00671805

A version of the Backyard-Hen Fantasy section was published on the Free from Harm website on May 11, 2014, as "Backyard Chickens: Expanding Our Understanding of 'Harm.'"

Published by:
Vegan Publishers
Danvers, MA
www.veganpublishers.com

Cover photo by Joey deVilla
Cover and text design by Nicola May Design

Printed in the United States of America

ISBN: 9781940184340

CONTENTS

FOREWORD
Carol J. Adams

Animal advocates often wonder: Why don't people get that animals suffer, that their suffering matters to them and us, that an alternative way of relating to animals exists, and that this alternative way is not constraining but liberating? In this book, Robert Grillo offers an answer to these questions. He identifies the structures and institutions that allow people to *not get it*, and that confirm people in their not getting it.

Ideological systems often screen humans from animal harm and suffering by offering legitimizing rationalizations for those harms. Robert has devoted his work to detailing these ideological systems. He wants us to understand how "popular culture uses a set of fictions and fictional devices" to shape our beliefs and perceptions about farmed animals. Back in 1992, Brian Luke called these fictions "industry cover stories."[1] As Robert details, we are bombarded with evolutionary fictions, humane-washing, victim denial, and trivialization, among many other cover stories. Myths of our superiority and the animals' inferiority, myths of animals' consent to their treatment, myths that naturalize and normalize the unnatural and the cruel all insulate individuals from getting it. He reminds us of language's power to hide or expose the truth. The prevalence of euphemisms like *harvesting* that substitute for *killing* in animal agriculture tells us they choose hiding the truth. He shows how, over a lifetime, we've come to accept this fictional world as fact. But more than just acceptance, we unknowingly project this fictional reality back out to our social world and actively defend it when it is challenged.

The vast majority of consumers trust those who profit from animals' bodies to police themselves. The people interpreting what is tolerable and permissible are those with a vested interest in making a profit on the bodies under their control. Robert reminds us that "farmers are not experts in animal behavior." He exposes the double standard of anthropomorphism: animal agriculture wants us to believe animals are "pampered," projecting a notion of comfort according to human standards (and, I would add, depicting animals as females who desire to be consumed—another form of anthropomorphism). Yet their charge against animal advocates is that *we* are anthropomorphic!

All of these ways of pummeling thoughts and reactions to animals to fit into a narrow sphere of unconcern are devised to keep us from caring. In another important article, published in 1996, Brian Luke argues that it is not that people don't care, it is that people do care, but they have been fragmented and are unable "to recognize [their] sympathies as a potential basis for action." He offers the example of wanting to eat a lobster. Years earlier, he had learned that he must drop the lobster into boiling water and found this task very distressing. He imagined being boiled alive. Yet he executed the steps needed to boil the lobster alive. Reflecting on this in his article, he writes, "It is not that I considered sparing the lobster but decided against it; rather, *the possibility never occurred to me*, even though I sweated and agonized over the suffering I expected to inflict."[2] Let's assume caring is intrinsic to our moral being and at the same time that fictions and ideological screens operate on us the way they did on Brian—preventing us from responding to our caring, equipping us, against ourselves, to be unable to use our care as a basis for moral action.

All the methods Robert uncovers show us the enormous efforts required—the economic and social structures, the advertisements, the cultural context—to keep the lies alive. Maybe the tactics and fictions and efforts Robert exposes exist because they have to work against the reality that people actually do care. Once we are liberated to employ our caring selves to reject the cover stories, we see that caring is not only an appropriate response to the information the animal industry wishes to keep from us, it is the most appropriate response.

At the heart of veganism is compassion: we care about the lives of animals. Through experience, education, or intuition, we recognize that our relationships include other animals and that these relationships inflict pain and suffering on nonhuman others by requiring their bodies to feed, cloth, or entertain us. Vegans realize that our decisions about what we eat, wear, and use exploits other animals and that it is possible to refuse to participate in this exploitation. In *Yonnondio: From the Thirties*, the writer Tillie Olsen refers to the "vanishing entire for harmless creatures meek and mild, frisky, wild."[3] Vegans care about this vanishing entire and are trying to stop it.

Without this language of care, we don't have the best ax to cut through the excuses and normalizations and naturalizations that have iced over care. The ice ax that is needed is perhaps not argumentative but inviting, recognizing that people haven't lost the ability to care—they need to learn how to align it with actions. We cut through the structures to resituate care.

The feminist ethics of care rejects abstract rule-based ethics and sees animals as individuals who have feelings, who can communicate those feelings, and to whom therefore humans have moral obligations. An ethic of care also recognizes the diversity of animals—one size doesn't fit all; each has a particular history. Insofar as possible, attention needs to be paid to these particularities in any ethical determination regarding them. Attention is a key word in feminist ethic-of-care theorizing about animals. *Attention* to the individual suffering animal but also attention to the political and economic systems that are causing the suffering. Robert helps us understand these systems.

Ethic-of-care theorists emphasize that our attention be directed as well to what the animals are telling us—rather than what other humans are telling us. In 1990, Josephine Donovan called for a renewed emphasis on dialogue with animals, learning their communication systems, reading their body language phenomenologically, and taking these communications seriously in our ethical decisions.[4]

As I was finishing this preface, social media was alive with the story of a mother goose who went up to a police car. The policeman, James Givens, explained what happened next:

> "This goose came up and started pecking on the side of the car," Givens told The Dodo. "I threw some food out for her, but she didn't take it. She just kept pecking and quacking. Then she walked away, stopped and looked back. Then came over again and pecked some more."
>
> When the goose walked away a second time, and again looked back, Givens decided to follow her.[5]

When Givens followed the goose, he found her gosling all tangled up in a balloon string. A policewoman arrived to help, and after a few minutes disentangled the baby as the mother goose waited. Once released, the gosling and the mother goose headed to the lake.

Many of the hundreds of thousands of people posting the video that shows the last few minutes of the untangling of the balloon have probably eaten dead goose, or exclaimed over foie gras. They've accepted the ideological screens. But here's a new Mother Goose story. Not built on industry fictions, euphemisms, and lies, but by paying attention to what animals are saying and doing.

Peck-peck-peck: the animals, themselves, give the lie to the cover stories.

Peck-peck-peck: the beak knocks on our conscience.

Peck-peck-peck: as Robert equips us, let us remove the victim-blaming, the fictions, the submissive acceptance of farmers' interpretations.

Peck-peck-peck: freeing ourselves from the entanglements of industry lies and distortions allows us to be allies with the animals seeking their own freedom.

It is possible to *get it*.

PREFACE

As a young man in my late twenties, I got my start in the publishing field at a small business publisher where I learned typesetting and design for newsletters and books. With an English and communications major, I planned on pursuing a career in the publishing industry, but I soon realized that working as a freelancer for creative agencies was more lucrative and exciting. I could put the skills I learned in publishing to use and bill a higher rate as well. So, for several years, I picked up freelance gigs at various advertising and creative agencies. At one long-term assignment, I found myself working on McDonald's Happy Meal boxes and Kraft Foods brand packaging and signage. I never once saw the problem with the portrayal of happy animals on the package containing the body parts of other animals who lived miserable lives. And it never occurred to me at the time how this branding was intentionally sending mixed messages to children. I later realized that it is this very disconnect between the animals on the package and the animals inside the package that serves as the flimsy foundation for the immeasurable suffering we cause. And it inundates us from birth to death.

It wasn't until 2009, after an impulsive move to adopt three chicks, that I began to question all my assumptions about food and animals. I named them Doris, Danita, and Riccardo, three of nineteen chicks born to a chick-hatching project at a school where a friend of mine taught. When I adopted them, I knew nothing about caring for chickens. I taught myself everything I needed to know online. I bonded with them and they with me immediately, and I grew to love them and regard them as members of our family. Soon they were following me around the house, cuddling up in my lap, and doing everything that companion animals like cats and dogs do.

And an interesting thing happened: the more I got to know these birds, the wider the gulf became between what I had been taught and what I was now learning. I found myself forced to grapple with two starkly different realities: the new reality based on my real-life, first-hand experiences with these birds and the old reality, the fictional world perpetuated by popular culture, the world you and I were taught to accept without question because this worldview also stifles critical thinking. In the stark contrast between this new and old reality lies the truth about animals, about ourselves, about our relationship with other animals, and about our rightful place in the natural world to which we belong, a world from which we've become completely estranged. And this estrangement, this detachment, is the source of many of our most pressing problems today. It is the source of our conflicts, not only with other animals, but with other human groups and with the environment upon which our survival and well-being depends.

This is a book about how popular culture uses a set of fictions and fictional devices to shape our beliefs and perceptions of farmed animals (as well as the products derived from their bodies) and manipulate the food choices that stem from those beliefs. I hope to show that the engine behind this cultural indoctrination is largely animal-agriculture branding, which props up a fictional world so entrenched in our minds that we stopped questioning it long ago—a fictional world that tells us what we want to hear, shows us what we want to see, and ultimately reflects back upon us what we want to believe. It's as if our minds have switched into autopilot. Our everyday existence is immersed in this fictional world at every turn, from the moment we get up and turn on the radio or TV or reach for the dairy milk or egg carton until we finally turn everything off and retire to bed. Over a lifetime, we've come to accept this fictional world as "fact." But more than just acceptance, we unknowingly project this fictional reality back out to our social world and actively defend it when it is challenged. This book is about taking a long overdue and much-needed critical look at the fictions we've been fed.

ACKNOWLEDGMENTS

This book is the culmination of years of questioning how our culture conditions us to consume animals, thereby contributing to an immense underworld of suffering. As the director of Free from Harm, I've been fortunate to attract a remarkably talented team to assist me on this book. I'd like to thank Samyuktha Iyer, who assisted me in research; Carla Black Vissers, who provided editorial guidance to help sharpen my voice; and Ernesto Melchor-Alonso and Nancy Flood, who helped me fact check, research sources, and compile footnotes. I extend a very special thank you to Ashley Capps, co-editor and writer of Free from Harm, whose honest advice and insights I find continually invaluable. Her heart, intellect, ideas, and sentiment are infused throughout this book. I am grateful to Carol Adams for not just writing a wonderful foreword, but also for taking an in-depth interest in my book and offering me her perspective on writing style and the book's structure. I am forever grateful to my family and my partner, Tom, who has offered his support on so many levels. I must also thank Vegan Publishers for being the catalyst for me to write the book and to their wonderful editor Nicole Brugger-Dethmers for her fresh perspective and comprehensive editing and proofreading. And, finally, a huge thanks to all of the visionaries in the world of social justice who inspire us to always forge ahead!

Chapter 1:

Why We Believe

As children, most of us are taught to treat animals with respect and kindness. Even when we are presented with living farmed animals at, say, a petting zoo, the adult world provides clear moral guidelines for how to interact with these animals, including what is acceptable behavior and what is not. The same is true for all of our other public encounters with animals. But then we return home from a day at the petting zoo and our parents serve us the very animals we were taught to respect when alive at the petting zoo. Some children are rightfully confused by this contradiction and understandably ask questions. The response from the adult world contradicts what they taught us at the petting zoo. When we ask about why we are eating these animals, adults have a wide range of explanations that all essentially lead to one conclusion: *you don't need to care.* This sentiment is expressed through common explanations like "It's part of the natural cycle," "It's just the way things are," "That's what they're here for," "Grow up," or "Toughen up." Our childhood confusion stems from the startling hypocrisy of this message: We must respect animals during the short time they are allowed to stay alive, but we don't need to respect their very lives? When people are prompted with the question of whether they were taught not to care, often more and more memories and stories that were stored away come to the surface.

As we will explore later on in the book, most children appear to be born with an innate empathy for all animals. They learn prejudice and discrimination based on race, sex, and species from the adult world. This phenomenon demonstrates how powerful cultural and social pressures lead us to go against what's in our hearts, especially when it comes to the animals we eat. And even more startling is how widespread and consistent this phenomenon is in all of the animal-eating cultures. So how can this conditioning work so well on so many of us for so long?

CONSIDERING *THE MATRIX*
This question is central to the film *The Matrix*. While most narratives from popular culture are carefully crafted around what we

want to see, hear, and believe, *The Matrix* asks us to question what we've been taught, to separate what is illusion from what is real, what is oppression from what is freedom. And *The Matrix* is all the more important because of its notoriety as a "cult classic." In the film, Morpheus explains to Neo that the Matrix is a simulated reality based on what the world was like in 1999, into which harvested humans are pacified and trapped as slaves by the sentient machines of their own creation. Morpheus and his followers make up a rebel group who hack into the Matrix and "unplug" enslaved humans and recruit them as rebels. Morpheus becomes convinced that Neo is "the One" prophesied to end the war between humans and machines. In one defining moment, he offers Neo a choice to take the red pill or the blue pill, explaining that taking the red pill will reveal the truth about reality. When Neo chooses the red pill, Morpheus then explains what the Matrix means:

> Morpheus: The Matrix is everywhere. It is all around us. Even now, in this very room. You can see it when you look out your window or when you turn on your television. You can feel it when you go to work . . . when you go to church . . . when you pay your taxes. It is the world that has been pulled over your eyes to blind you from the truth.

> Neo: What truth?

> Morpheus: That you are a slave, Neo. Like everyone else you were born into bondage, into a prison that you cannot taste or see or touch. A prison for your mind.[1]

An important message in *The Matrix* is that the way out of our mental prison starts with seeking and skepticism, which require a certain amount of courage and humility in admitting that we may have been misled. And if we open our minds, we might even overcome our denial and defenses to face hidden truths. Animal advocacy, like other social justice movements, asks us to confront difficult realities, but the ultimate reward goes to those who have the courage to witness because seeing things as they really are liberates us from oppression. Silence and denial keep oppression alive, and breaking that silence and denial disempowers it. While *The Matrix* doesn't necessarily relate to liberating animals from the suffering we impose upon them, its message is universal enough to apply to both humans and other species.

The Matrix grapples with the uncomfortable fact that most of us choose the blue pill (fiction) over the red pill (fact). In terms of eating animals, taking the blue pill serves two important functions: First, taking the blue pill reinforces what we want to see, hear, and believe. We want to believe that farmed animals, at least for the short time they are permitted to remain alive, are treated with respect and suffer minimally on that "one bad day." Second, taking the blue pill advances the agenda of the animal exploitation industries by presenting animals as willing participants in whatever it is we want to do with them. Social psychologist Melanie Joy refers to the Matrix that is carnism, a term she uses to identify the belief system of eating animals.[2] For meat-eating cultures around the world, carnism is so entrenched that it remains an invisible Matrix most people don't think or talk about. "It's just the way things are," Joy often points out. By identifying and critiquing carnism, we break through the myth that only vegans and vegetarians eat according to a certain set of beliefs. For Joy, carnism remains a dominant belief system to the extent that it remains unquestioned, shrouded in silence and protected by collective denial.

STORYTELLING, CULTURE, AND POWER

Nearly all of the fictions and fictional devices abundant in popular culture today in relation to eating animals have ancient roots. Even before we had written languages, oral storytelling existed for millennia as a way of embedding important ideas in compelling stories. The goal was to make the stories interesting enough so that young people would find them worth passing on to the next generation. Etchings, illustrations, and other forms of art, architecture, and monuments supported these stories and endowed them with a powerful visual language. Today storytelling remains our greatest tool of persuasion, especially when coupled with modern information technologies like social media, e-mail, texting, video monitors, digital signage, and the all-encompassing retail experience.

In the modern age, political theorist and strategist Antonio Gramsci made enduring contributions to our understanding of the intersection between storytelling, culture, and power. Gramsci grew up under the fascist rule of Benito Mussolini. As an outspoken critic of fascism and head of the Italian Communist Party, Gramsci was imprisoned by Mussolini and spent much time writing in his prison cell. In fact, he wrote thousands of pages of manuscript which would later be regarded as some of the most important work on political theory and strategy to come out of the era, influencing many important social movements to this day. Among the many ideas for which he is renown, just one serves our purpose here: cultural hegemony. Cultural hegemony is the domination and manipulation of a society's norms, habits, customs, values, and beliefs through propaganda (stories and fictions that promote the worldview of the dominant class). This worldview is imposed and eventually accepted as the cultural norm and the basis for justifying the social, political, and economic status quo as natural, inevitable, perpetual, and beneficial for everyone, rather than as artificial social constructs that benefit only the ruling class.[3] In some respects, it is what we innocuously refer to today as popular culture.

Gramsci observed that fascism wielded absolute power, not just in terms of brute force, but also through cultural hegemony, through propaganda built upon powerful fictions. One infamous example is the program that became known as "mercy killing" or "euthanasia." The 1986 documentary *Paradise Camp* tells the infamous story of how the Nazi concentration camp in Czechoslovakia known as Theresienstadt was cleaned up in preparation for a visit from the International Red Cross. The Nazis themselves filmed a documentary showing Jewish and Roma child prisoners looking well-dressed, clean, smiling, and singing patriotic songs. This was the image of Nazism they wanted the world to see. The reality was that these children were living in squalor and would soon be exterminated.[4]

A modern day example of cultural hegemony and one that is strikingly similar to the fascist example is humane-washing, which will be covered in much greater detail later in this book. Humane-washing surrounds us wherever animal products are marketed and sold, presenting us with feel-good images of happy animals and their benevolent caretakers and crafting feel-good fictions about happy animals, happy about being exploited, happy to be sacrificed to satisfy our taste sensations. Of course, the reality is that their lives are drastically and violently cut short in infant or adolescent age by those who profit on their bodies. In both cases, propaganda is successfully used to conceal the systematic violence against and oppression of an inferior group who are "sacrificed" in the name of some benefit to a superior group.

In the end, Gramsci argued that the cultural hegemony of an oppressive regime can only be defeated through a counterhegemonic movement that successfully embarks on a "war of position" through a prolonged intellectual, cultural, and moral confrontation over contemporary common sense conceptions of reality, a process of winning over the masses by consent and through education. In our case, the contemporary "common sense" that needs to be challenged is that notion that other animals are here for us to exploit and that it's okay to exploit them however we choose.

THE POWER OF FOOD FICTIONS

Finally, in understanding why we believe so deeply and completely in popular culture's fictions about farmed animals, we must consider the power of money. While this fictional world surrounds us every day, its genius lies in how well it camouflages itself. This helps hide the fact that animal agriculture spends an enormous amount of money to keep these fictions alive in our consciousness. In other words, it costs a lot of money to keep us from questioning the fundamental disconnect between not wanting animals to suffer gratuitously and yet ignoring the 99 percent we gratuitously harm to satisfy our taste buds. So how much money does this take? In the 2012 fiscal year, Cargill, one of the largest entities in animal agriculture, spent $1.792 billion just on promoting animal products to consumers. In contrast, the Humane Society of the United States spent just a portion of its $126.36 million budget to help farmed animals in 2010.[5] But it is not just the agriculture sector that spends so lavishly on managing our perceptions of them. A system of government subsidies and marketing might has become a key part of the equation to help keep animal exploitation profitable. Through the Agricultural Marketing Service (AMS), the United States Department of Agriculture's stated mission is to "facilitate the competitive and efficient marketing of agricultural products in domestic and international markets, while ensuring fair trading practices."[6] And one key strategy is "promoting a strategic marketing perspective that adapts product and marketing decisions to consumer demands. . . ."[7] In other words, the AMS helps agriculture create the fictional world that keeps us taking the blue pill. To this end, the AMS effectively budgeted $1.332 billion in 2013 to the agricultural sector just for marketing assistance alone.[8] This does not include the billions of dollars in subsidies awarded each year to the same sector.

Set against the stark reality of animals reduced to agricultural commodities, the next chapter will look at what we actually know about the rich and complex lives of farmed animals, according to the latest scientific discoveries as well as powerful anecdotal evidence from caregivers and sanctuaries where these animals are allowed to express their true natures.

Chapter 2:

Facing the
Animal Facts

Before exploring how fictions and fictional devices are used to mislead us about animals and condition us to feel good about eating them, let's briefly look at some recent discoveries from scientific and observational study that require us to completely re-evaluate who farmed animals really are. But, even here, the science is often funded by animal agriculture and is therefore steeped in the prejudices and misconceptions from popular culture. It's important to consider the source and objectives of a study. In browsing the research, we will find many examples where animal testing and biological manipulation that force animals to secrete more milk or lay more eggs or grow faster flesh tissue are almost always portrayed in a positive light, while ignoring the suffering they inflict. Studying an animal under the controlled and unnatural conditions in which they are used as economic commodities will not likely result in anything meaningful or realistic about the animal's true nature. On the contrary, such studies "feed into the culture that regards it as acceptable to exploit them," says Sandra Higgins, director of Eden Farm Animal Sanctuary in Ireland, in an e-mail dated June 23, 2013.

A prime example is "The Intelligent Hen Study," sponsored by the Happy Egg Co.—a company which, incidentally, just a few years prior, was the subject of a major undercover animal cruelty investigation filmed in 2010 by the United Kingdom–based vegan charity Viva!.[9] Happy Egg Co. hired the University of Bristol to carry out a study to "inform range and enrichment design on its farms." So the overall intention of the study was narrowly focused on how to improve the welfare of hens already bred to produce eggs on commercial farms. Yet, by studying them under the very conditions that inhibit their ability to express their true nature, the study is compromised by its very design, ignoring all of the suffering endured as a result of commodification and centuries of selective breeding and undermining any serious attempt to understand their authentic behavior or intelligence. Christine Nicol, professor of animal welfare at the University of Bristol and a twenty-year veteran researcher of chickens, who co-authored the study with Robbie l'Anson-Price, said the findings point to "the importance of providing these amazing creatures with the environment that enables them to live out their natural instincts."[10] However, if this statement has any meaning whatsoever, it most certainly means that raising chickens for commercial purposes—a purpose that has nothing to do with expressing the animal's natural inclinations—conflicts with an "environment that enables them to live out their natural instincts." Indeed, even so-called humane farms systematically deny them all or most of the conditions under which they could perform their natural behavior.

WHAT THE SCIENCE CAN TELL US

Fortunately, there is a growing body of science motivated by an interest in understanding animals for their own sake. For example, in 2012, the Cambridge Declaration on Consciousness was published and signed by 400 of the world's leading cognitive neuroscientists.[11] This broad statement about human and nonhuman cognition nevertheless represents a sharp break with the past and challenges key flaws in centuries of scientific research about animal consciousness. The Declaration states that

> convergent evidence indicates that non-human animals have the neuroanatomical, neurochemical, and neurophysiological substrates of conscious states along with the capacity to exhibit intentional behaviors. Consequently, the weight of evidence indicates that humans are not unique in possessing the neurological substrates that generate consciousness. Non-human animals, including all mammals and birds, and many other creatures, including octopuses, also possess these neurological substrates.[12]

In the first study of its kind, researchers at the University of Chicago have demonstrated that rats engage in empathy-driven behavior, helping to free a trapped cage mate for no reward other than relieving his cage mate's distress.[13] Although previous research has suggested that empathy isn't the exclusive province of humans, this is the first study to show such prosocial behavior in rodents. Researchers say the basic understanding of empathy in lower animals could help scientists understand better how empathy functions in humans, and even increase it in humans. "It's a neat new experimental procedure that may facilitate the empirical understanding of empathy," says Jaak Panksepp, a pioneer in the study of emotions in animals.[14] In the study, rats chose to help each other out of traps, even when distracted by a stash of delicious chocolate chips. Researchers observed that the free rats immediately liberated their trapped partners, once they figured out how to open the restraint. In certain cases, they persevered up to a week before succeeding. Rats that were exposed to empty restrainers or a trapped toy rat ignored them. "They are very smart and figure out if they pitch their nose up, they can open the door," writes Jean Decety, one of the researchers. "It's not easy and it doesn't happen by chance. They try hard and circle around."[15] The researchers did not teach the rats how to nudge the door open or give them any incentive to do so. Even when opening the door would release their companions into a separate compartment, rats freed each other.

According to the organization Fish Feel, fish are the largest category of exploited animals, are subjected to arguably the worst abuses, and receive the least advocacy and protection.[16] In a report published in 2010, the European organization Fishcount took on the enormously complex challenge of trying to quantify the number of fish caught and killed for food on a global scale based on data from the Food and Agriculture Organization of the United Nations (FAO). According to their data, each year 970–2,700 billion fish are caught from the wild and 37–120 billion farmed fish are raised and killed for food.[17] For wild fish, an astonishing 40 percent is bycatch—what the industry refers to as the animals who are unintentionally captured, the nontarget prey.[18] The World Wildlife Fund reports that these collateral victims include over 300,000 small whales, dolphins, and porpoises, over 250,000 endangered loggerhead turtles and critically endangered leatherback turtles, and as many as 320,000 seabirds.

Meanwhile, the evidence is mounting on fish sentience and intelligence. One leading fish researcher, Donald Broom, professor of animal welfare at Cambridge University, tells us that "the scientific literature is quite clear. Anatomically, physiologically and biologically, the pain system in fish is virtually the same as in birds and mammals."[19] But beyond just sentience and ability to feel pain, other leading scientists such as Culum Brown, associate professor at Macquarie University, claim that "in many areas, such as memory, their cognitive powers match or exceed those of 'higher' vertebrates, including non-human primates. Best of all, given the central place memory plays in intelligence and social structures, fish not only recognize individuals but can also keep track of complex social relationships."[20]

Tragically, our new-found knowledge about fish has had little impact on public perceptions, let alone on how commercial fisheries ruthlessly exploit them. Fishcount explains that "most wild-caught fish are likely to die from being crushed in nets or from suffocation, freezing or live dissection after landing. This process will probably take many minutes, or even hours. Most of the world's farmed fish are also killed by slow and inhumane methods."[21] In a 2012 Animal Equality investigation of standard tuna fishing off of the coast of Sardinia, investigators found a horrifying bloodbath where "fish were dragged from the ocean with giant sharp metal pick hooks and brought on-board ships. Extensive tissue damage was caused by the piercing [from these] blunt hooks, and this is likely to have inflicted acute pain on the fish, who were still alive and conscious."[22] Once hoisted upon boat docks, video footage shows these majestic tuna being viciously stabbed with harpoons as they thrash helplessly in their last remaining moments of life. Meanwhile, a new market is emerging for so-called humane and sustainable fish and seafood alternatives, but much like their counterparts in the flesh, dairy, and egg industries, the humane standards are short on substance and are misleading through the marketing of these products. For example, Fishcount tells us that clubbing fish over the head to stun them is touted as the humane alternative to letting them suffocate to death on ship decks and gutting them while still conscious and their hearts are still beating. In a promotional video from Wild Salmon Direct, the narrator explains, "A percussive blow to the head humanely kills each fish,"[23] while showing salmon frantically trying to escape as they are sucked into a machine that clubs them on the head to knock them unconscious.

Contrary to popular belief, studies since 1995 confirm that the avian brain is a complex organ comparable to that of mammals. An article in *Science Daily* called "Bird Brain? Birds and Humans Have Similar Brain Wiring" concludes that birds possess complex social reasoning and problem solving, among many other previously unrecognized cognitive abilities. A researcher explains that "birds have been evolving separately from mammals for around 300 million years," yet they are "remarkably intelligent in a similar way to mammals such as humans and monkeys."[24] What we've learned about the chicken, and the avian brain and behavior in general, in just the last fifteen years contradicts hundreds of years of misconceptions about chickens and other birds. Much of what was previously thought to be the exclusive domain of human/primate communication, brain and cognitive function, and social behavior is now being discovered in chickens and other birds. It's nothing short of a revolution in our understanding of chickens. The science is confirming what many who have observed chickens closely for years have long since witnessed: chickens are far more intelligent and cognitively sophisticated than previously believed. While intelligence level is not a morally relevant criterion for how we treat others, these findings can help us debunk long-standing prejudices and harmful stereotypes about chickens that contribute to their utterly abysmal status in our society. In fact, chickens and turkeys combined represent 98–99 percent of all animals killed for food in the United States. Some 8.7 billion chickens in the United States and some 40 billion globally are slaughtered each year at around six weeks of age.[25]

One of the most striking discoveries is that the modern domesticated chicken has much in common with the wild jungle fowl from which he descends. New Zealand–based animal studies scholar and author Annie Potts explains that "despite the different circumstances between wild and domestic fowl, their behaviours, when permitted natural expression, remain very similar."[26] This contradicts the common belief that natural behaviors and desires have been essentially "bred out" of the domestic chicken.[27]

A recent high-profile study of chicken behavior by Christine Nicol credits chickens with the ability to perform complex skills within days of hatching, such as basic arithmetic, self control, and basic structural engineering—skills that don't develop in humans until their toddler years. The mass media turned these comparisons into catchy headlines like "Can chickens REALLY be cleverer than a toddler?" Ethologist Giorgio Vallortigara of the University of Trento, Italy, is widely recognized as a pioneer in chicken behavior and cognition research, specifically with newly hatched chicks. His work demonstrates how chicks are born with an understanding of basic arithmetic, geometry, and physics; advanced problem-solving; and quick learning and retention. Italian psychologists Rosa Rugani, Lucia Regolin, and Vallortigara have shown that chicks prefer to join groups of more objects over a single object or a smaller set of objects. The chicks in these studies were found to imprint with these objects as if they were their mothers or flock mates. As the researchers explain, "the most complex numerical ability is to manipulate numbers by performing simple arithmetic. We know rhesus monkeys can do this and we know that five-day-old chicks can too."[28] In the National Museum of Animals & Society's exhibit *Uncooped*, Vallortigara explains that his purpose for studying young domestic chicks is to investigate the origins of knowledge; I'm interested in core knowledge abilities like number, space, time and cause, and I am trying to clarify how much of these abilities are already available at birth, before interactions with objects of the world may have shaped them through learning and experience. We found that indeed newly hatched chicks do possess surprisingly sophisticated abilities at birth, they know about basic principles of physics (such as solidity), could perform basic arithmetic (with small numerousness), [and] they can deal with the geometry of enclosed surfaces to orient and navigate.[29]

LEARNING FROM OPEN-MINDED OBSERVATION

While science provides important empirical validation to our understanding of animal intelligence and behavior, anyone with an inquisitive mind and an interest in farmed animals can learn a great deal about them just by observing and interacting with them. In a safe and trusting environment free of expectations on them to produce something, farmed animals quickly reveal their individual personalities. The internet is full of stories, photos, and videos of people who have found deep companionship with their rescued farmed animals. A growing number of individual caretakers, rescuers, and sanctuaries raise chickens, turkeys, cows, and pigs and are learning a great deal from them as individuals.

Those who have visited a sanctuary can attest to how fundamentally different the experience is from visiting a farm. On a sanctuary, animals are recognized as self-aware individuals who, like human beings, have unique personalities—a complex of experiences, interests, emotions, thoughts, memories, likes, dislikes, desires, fears, friends, loves, losses, joys, and pains. Property owners are replaced with guardians who provide a caring environment that empowers them with the confidence to more authentically express their true selves. And sanctuaries, while still imperfect, manmade environments, strive to provide their inhabitants with as natural a life as possible. People can walk away from sanctuaries with a "breakthrough" understanding. They recognize that these individuals are vastly more expressive, more sophisticated than their repressed counterparts on farms. They see much of themselves in these animals. They realize that the stereotypes they've come to believe all of their lives are based on an inherent and deeply entrenched cultural prejudice.

Visiting animals on farms, in contrast, does not produce any "breakthrough" in our understanding of animals because the objective of farms is not to provide an environment in which animals are free to express themselves or an environment where animals can be studied and better understood. Farmers are not experts in animal behavior, and they are not even necessarily good observers of animals. In fact, many farmers deny that animals suffer under routine farming practices and a violent death. Under the very best circumstances, farms provide an understanding of how animals subsist under completely manmade, controlled conditions, as if their fate as commodities is a foregone conclusion. As a result, most visitors to farms walk away reaffirming what they've already been taught, that animals don't object to being used as resources since it's all they know. On farms, we often view meek or fearful animals from a distance or on the other side of an electrical fence, typically in herds or flocks with ear tags (numbers instead of names), and under conditions that repress their ability to express themselves as individuals. Even farmers who claim to love their animals like family members still regard them as *utility* animals, as dictated by the economics of that human-property relationship. In the words of former pig farmer and writer Bob Comis, "livestock farmers, no matter what kind — from the largest, most cynical, and inhumane factory farmers to the smallest, seemingly most ethical pasture-based farmers — traffic in death. It is death that is our aim, our purpose. Death is the end. Life is the means. Money the reward."[30]

On sanctuaries, individual animals often have storied lives marked by abuse or neglect. They are the survivors whose suffering would have been ignored and whose lives would have been in vain, had it not been for sanctuaries and rescuers. Sanctuaries challenge visitors with a new paradigm for understanding animals. They present their adopted and rescued residents as they are and ask us to observe and interact with them as unique individuals, rather than by the norms, assumptions, and prejudices imposed upon their species by thousands of years of exploitation. For sanctuaries, animals are in fact an end in themselves, rather than a means to an end.[31]

Chapter 3

The Foundational Fictions

In the constellation of fictions described in this book, there are a handful of fictions that we can identify as foundational because they serve as the building blocks for creating more elaborate narratives that combine other fictional devices for more powerful effect. But before we look at these in more detail, there's a common question that arises from the examples presented in this chapter that is worth addressing up front. Many have asked, "Why not focus on the largest corporate exploiters and just leave the small producers of animal products alone?" There's no dispute that large corporate entities have the greatest concentration of money, power, and influence to inflict the most suffering on animals based on the sheer scale of their enterprises. Yet, long before so-called modern factory farms existed, the model for large-scale animal commodification was actually established in early civilizations, as evidenced by inventions like the artificial incubator in ancient Egypt.

Consequently, this book seeks to demonstrate just how deeply these fictions permeate our culture, far beyond modern agribusiness. In fact, it would be misleading to conclude that these fictions are somehow exclusive to corporate branding, nor do they even necessarily originate there. It is critical that we understand that they have much deeper cultural and historical roots. So embedded are they in our culture that many people no longer recognize them, let alone question where they originate or who continues to perpetuate them. They are steeped in the language of celebrated writers and great works of literature, in the moving images of iconic films, in the work of some of the most iconic artists and musicians, and in the adventures of popular nature, travel, and cooking shows, just to name a few. Most importantly, they embody the dominant worldview held by all of our important social institutions, such as the schools where we send our children, the doctors and hospitals we trust with our health, the government agencies that determine our dietary guidelines, the companies where we are employed, and even the nonprofits that we support to advance important social justice causes. We assimilate this fictional paradigm and project it back out to our own social network of family, friends, and acquaintances. And so the feedback loop continues.

ANTHROPOMORPHISM

One of the most striking examples of anthropomorphism is a TV commercial featuring Jim Perdue talking about what good lives his chickens have. The scene cuts to the interior of a chicken coop where chickens are facing stage mirrors with the little white ball lights around them, as if to suggest they are getting ready to go on stage and give a performance. And people believe that this reflects some truth, albeit a whimsical twist on the truth, about chickens in Perdue's care. A neighbor once said he had heard that chickens were actually very well cared for. He probably arrived at this belief from seeing this or some similar commercial, and the fiction became embedded in his consciousness, never to seek questioning again. That's how a good fiction works. It stifles any further critical thinking on the subject. In fact, no one ever seems to have a problem when a major food brand like Perdue uses anthropomorphism in its advertising to mislead us into believing that its chickens are actually pampered. It just so happens to be right in line with what we want to hear, see, and believe about how they are raised, so instead of evaluating the claim critically, we accept it at face value. But then as soon as some dissenting view surfaces that challenges our massive system of animal exploitation, we are quick to level accusations of anthropomorphism for attributing human traits to other animals.

In a recent discussion on YouTube, a pig farmer/veterinarian accused others of being anthropomorphic for stating that pigs suffer by being enslaved and confined, but then she used a counteranthropomorphic defense by claiming that no one could prove to her that her pigs weren't content. Her claim is anthropomorphic because it assumes that she understands what her pigs are thinking and feeling about being confined and commodified, and that they would not prefer to live free of confinement and on their own terms, if given the choice. She is not an animal behaviorist or other kind of scientist, nor did she bring any scientific or other credible evidence to support her claim. She is projecting what she assumes to know about her pigs, specifically that they don't mind confinement because they've never known freedom, and this claim conveniently fits her agenda for exploiting them for her own gain. But just because they have never known freedom doesn't prove that they prefer confinement over freedom.

Anthropomorphism—the attribution of human characteristics or behavior to another species—is the thread that weaves together many of the fictions and fictional devices that follow in this book. The exploiter's fictional executions portray farmed animals as expressing a range of positive emotions, or at least no negative reaction, in response to their enslavement by humans. It is therefore designated as one of the foundational fictions upon which other fictions are built. It is not, however, anthropomorphism itself that is necessarily fictional, but instead, it is the *intent* behind anthropomorphism that determines its truthful or fictional nature. For example, critics of animal advocacy often make invalid accusations of anthropomorphism even in response to legitimate and well-researched claims about animals expressing emotions or feelings or acting in a socially complex or empathic manner similar to humans. For evolutionary biologist Marc Bekoff, what he calls biocentric anthropomorphism[32] is a means of engaging in "rigorous science" through the inherently flawed and limited lens of human perception. As he explains, "the way human beings describe and explain the behavior of other animals is limited by the language they use to talk about things in general. By engaging in anthropomorphism—using human terms to explain animals' emotions or feelings—humans make other animals' worlds accessible to themselves."[33] In response to the widespread backlash from the scientific community, Bekoff asserts that "the only guard against the inappropriate use of anthropomorphism is knowledge, or the detailed study of the minds and emotions of animals."[34]

Author and activist Karen Davis meets such accusations of anthropomorphism with some illuminating insights that emphasize the importance of intention:

> Anthropomorphism based on empathy and careful observation is a valid approach to understanding other species. After all, we can only see the world 'through their eyes' by looking through our own. The imposition of humanized traits and behaviors on other animals for purely selfish purposes, forcing them to behave in ways that are pathologic to the animals themselves, is not the same thing as drawing inferences about the emotions, interests, and desires of animals rooted in our common evolutionary heritage.[35]

Davis's reference to "anthropomorphism based on empathy and careful observation" brings to mind the powerful message of photojournalist Jo-Anne McArthur in the opening of Liz Marshall's film *The Ghosts in Our Machine* when she tells us that she feels like a war photographer documenting animals as if they are casualties of war. It seems apt to call it a war because, if humans were the casualties, it would most certainly be considered a war and an atrocity, both epic and endless, like no other in history. Protests would dwarf anything like those against the Vietnam War or the student movements of the 1960s. We call it a war because we know in our hearts and minds that what animals are experiencing is a systematic assault on their identities and bodies. You can see the horror and despair on their faces, in their agitated body language and movement, in their desperate calls and anxious, labored breath. Their communication beyond words is so visceral and so much like our own, it haunts us forever.

On the other hand, when animal exploiters attribute positive emotions to animals that they exploit for food (or other purposes) to downplay accusations of causing them to suffer, their position is not just erroneous from a scientific perspective; it's also transparently self-serving, conveniently portraying animals as "happy" to serve us, "happy" to make whatever sacrifice we demand of them. Indeed, anthropomorphism in this context is the foundation for some of the most powerful tools of persuasion in animal agriculture's arsenal: humane-washing and consent. Again, in the words of author and activist Karen Davis:

> In the rhetoric of exploitation—as opposed to the language of liberation—animals can be redeemed from being "just animals" only by being sacrificed to "higher" forms of life, via science, religion, entertainment, or edibility. Hence, whatever was or is done to them is justified by the "will" of the animals themselves. Nonhuman animals want to be raped, mutilated, imprisoned, and even murdered, if it will make them "higher" and more human-like, privileged to serve the human interest. This is the essence of false anthropomorphism and of the genocidal erasure of the animal's true identity in favor of the abuser's image.[36]

CONSENT

All too often, farmed animals are portrayed as willing participants in whatever it is we want to do with them. By portraying the relationship between farmer and the animals he exploits as consensual, we, as the consumers of his products, are misled into believing that other animals don't mind being used against their will, thereby reducing the issue to one of how we treat them. This has led not only to a wholesale denial of the value of their lives but also to a depraved standard of treatment we call "humane," which, if applied to our cats and dogs, would be considered torture and even sadism. And not only do we portray them as consensual, we embellish this fiction by portraying ourselves as their benevolent masters and protectors. We suggest that animals are elevated by the honor of serving us in exchange for our hard work in raising them, much like the honor bestowed upon a soldier who serves his country. Our language affirms this. We never say that we *take* their eggs, their secretions, their bodies, or their lives. Instead, we claim that they *give* them to us.

Fictional representations of consensual animal subjects precede recorded history itself and cross most cultural boundaries, which is not surprising since animals have been exploited for food for some ten thousand years or more. In Hinduism, in the popular depiction of Krishna milking the sacred cow, the cow willingly gives her milk to Krishna just as she would her own offspring. In this tradition's most important stories, the female lactating cow becomes both a symbolic and literal source of nourishment and mothering to the human race, as if to suggest that we need this maternal protection into our adult lives. The sacred Hindu cow is Mother Earth. In the ancient Vedic scriptures, Krishna describes the cow as she who elevates human civilization and connects us to the divine. Drinking her milk seems almost akin to drinking the blood of Jesus. The Indian cow sanctuary Shree Gopal Gaushala describes a symbiotic cow/human relationship in which

> the Cow is the most important animal for developing the human body to perfection. The body can be maintained by any kind of foodstuff, but Cow's milk is particularly essential for developing the finer tissues of the human brain so that one can understand the intricacies of transcendental knowledge. A civilized man is expected to live on foodstuffs comprising fruits, vegetables, grains, sugar and milk. The Bull helps in the agricultural process of producing grain, etc., and thus in one sense the Bull is the father of humankind, whereas the Cow is the Mother, for she supplies milk to human society. A civilized man is therefore expected to give all protection to the Bulls and Cows.[37]

In contemporary Western culture, a strikingly similar sentiment can be found in the branding of Organic Valley milk products. The carton design replaces Krishna with a benevolent family farmer affectionately petting a cow. In the modern twist on this narrative, cow's milk carries forward the ancient notion of nourishing us and giving us vigor and strength. And like the Vedic scriptures, modern-day marketing of dairy as essential to good health reinforces our dysfunctional dependence on drinking mother's baby formula as adults. Author Will Tuttle tells us that "we cannot bear the thought of growing up and leaving home. Perhaps we long for infancy and the peaceful oblivion of our mother's breast, and if hers isn't available, then we'll use the breast of any lactating mother, even if she's a cow and we have to kill her babies to get to it."[38]

Narratives and descriptions claiming that animals make sacrifices for us date back to our earliest recorded history and would have us believe that animals give their consent to being violently killed for a "greater good," such as to provide us with sustenance or at the request of a higher power. However, to sacrifice oneself means to exercise consent, to act freely, to make a conscious choice from a variety of circumstances. For example, upon seeing a woman being attacked on the street, we weigh the options of our next moves carefully in the interest of all parties concerned. We could go and call the police, or we could try to intervene and risk also being attacked. We may decide that the latter is a sacrifice we're willing to make because we feel compelled to act to save the victim. Another example is the soldier who, out of loyalty to his country, claims he is willing to sacrifice his life to defend his country. Even the most passive or symbolic sacrifice means that you consciously surrender, by choice, to another, perhaps to a loved one or to a higher power, in the form of worship or devotion.

But farmed animals who are exploited as resources are neither acting on their own free will, making a choice, or communicating their consent to being subjugated, enslaved, and killed. It is impossible to fairly describe such a situation as a sacrifice. What we do know for certain, based on observing their emotions and reactions, is that all animals, including ourselves, have a tenacious will to live and a willingness to go to great lengths to preserve their own lives, those of their immediate family, and even those of members of their extended social groups.

Even for indigenous people, who live on subsistence hunting and gathering and who kill animals for food out of necessity, the necessary act of killing does not constitute a sacrifice. Author and law professor Sherry Colb describes this as "a ritual of denial,"[39] a ritual intended to absolve the guilt one feels for having caused another sentient being harm. "Indigenous people — like us — created ways of coping with their own violence against animals through rituals of denial. Some indigenous hunters have given thanks to animals for gifts the animals never consented to bestow . . . ," writes Colb. "We have consumed the flesh and secretions of animals in restaurants carrying the names and images of ecstatic, celebrating versions of those same animals painted on the entrance."[40] Whether in the past or in the present, the notion that animals are willing to be harmed or killed as a sacrifice to us is not only anthropomorphic but also a powerful testament to how our remorse for inflicting suffering on others can drive us to deep levels of self-deception.

OBJECTIFICATION

Without objectification, animals cannot be reduced to products of consumption. In a farmers' market in Marin County, California—a mecca of organic agriculture and sustainability—one can purchase heritage-breed chicks from a cage full of newborn peeping chicks with a sign above their heads that reads "$2/each." Think about that for a moment. We place a monetary value on an entire lifetime of experiences that is less than the cost of a tube of toothpaste that will be thrown out within a matter of weeks. Even in this best-case scenario, we value these birds even less than everyday, disposable household objects, a value promulgated by the farming industry that has become accepted by society at large. Another way we can better understand objectification is to compare a wall-mounted beer bottle opener with the chick beak "trimmer" used by the egg industry that burns or severs the sensitive tip of a chick's beak. Not only do the two pieces of machinery have striking design similarities, but the callous way we handle the bottle and the chick are also the same. Objectification allows us to suspend moral or rational judgment so that we may erase any distinction between a beer bottle and a highly sentient and complex being. Without objectification, we are forced to recognize that chicks are incredibly precocious learners whose behavior has been studied intensely with the goal of shedding more light on how the human brain develops.

Moreover, the exploitation industries flood the media with images of objectified animals: handled like elements of production, confined to overcrowded quarters, hauled like cargo on trucks or planes, shackled by their legs, hung upside and hurled by machinery down a kill line—all grotesque misrepresentations of subjects transformed into objects. The intent of objectification is to infect us with apathy for the victims and annihilate the human or nonhuman animal identity, to transform what philosopher Tom Regan calls "subjects of a life"[41] —subjects who all share the same capacity for physical and emotional suffering—into usable and disposable objects. For animal law professor Lesli Bisgould, the fictionalized image of the animal object is normal to us by way of the long-standing property status of nonhuman animals. In legal terms, either one is legal property or a legal person worthy of rights to protect her from harm. And animals have, at the very least, a fundamental interest in not being violated, harmed, or otherwise made to suffer for our benefit. "If it seems strange to think of an animal as a legal person, consider that a whole array of inanimate constructs — corporations, churches, trusts, municipalities — are all legal persons in that they have legally protected interests and they can go to court and advance them," explains Bisgould in her TED Talk.[42] As pieces of property, fictionalized and fetishized objects of consumption, animals are denied the most fundamental right to life itself, which becomes the domain of whoever owns them.

SUPERIORITY

During the Q & A of a popular Intelligence Squared debate called "Why Animals Should Be Off the Menu," a very soft-spoken young man in the audience was given a chance to speak and had this to say:

> We are not carnivores. We eat meat by choice. Why would you choose to kill another animal and eat its flesh, when you could choose not to? I think meat feeds much more than our body; I think eating meat feeds our ego. Because by choosing to eat meat, we are demonstrating that we are powerful enough to dominate and kill other animals for reasons other than survival. We demonstrate it through technology on a farm where animals are kept in cages no matter how big or small. We demonstrate it through technology in an abattoir where animals are killed systematically by machines. Lastly and most importantly, we demonstrate it with our wallets where we pay top dollar for prime steak as a display of wealth. We are not carnivores. We eat meat by choice. And we choose to eat it to feed our ego.[43]

Most people agree with the following statements: "I'll always put a human before an animal" and "Humans are more important than animals." But even if we believe or could prove to be superior to other animals, in however we arbitrarily define our superiority, the fact that one feels superior to others does not justify exploiting, enslaving, killing, and eating them. A leading brain surgeon is not justified in violating someone with lower cognitive abilities or less education than himself, such as a patient who suffers from dementia. Even in cases where we may subjectively feel superior over someone else in competitions, there are strict rules to the game, and harming our competitors solely on the basis of feeling superior to them would be considered "playing dirty" and disqualify us. That's because we do not base morality on how well someone scores on an IQ test or how great an artist he is. The only morally relevant criterion for how we treat someone is whether they can suffer. All nonhuman animals qualify, since they visibly demonstrate fundamental interests in staying alive and avoiding pain, suffering, and death, not to mention a whole set of other complex interests that would be otherwise denied them.

But there is a deeper issue to explore in the human need to assert our superiority over other animals. Although we control the fate of the other animals on this planet, we still find it necessary to continually exert our self-professed superiority. Could it be that we are so deeply insecure about our alleged superiority—in relation to the other intelligent life forms on this planet that predate us by millions of years—that we feel compelled to continually remind ourselves how important we are? Is this desire to feel superior merely an expression of an inferiority complex? Is our understanding of our own intelligence—in relation to that of the other thousands of intelligent life forms we don't fully even understand—so myopic that our claim of superiority is akin to the tantrums of a spoiled child? Whatever the case, we act on this sense of superiority at every opportunity. The notion that human interests "trump" animal interests when we create an imaginary conflict of interest is particularly delusional when one considers that we wantonly kill sixty billion land animals and kill another trillion or so aquatic animals every year, not to protect any important human interest but just to suit our pleasure in eating them.

It's as if the all-powerful affirmation that humans are more important than other animals justifies anything we want to do to other animals, no matter how illogical, immoral, or destructive. But it seems that the only thing that is "superior" is our pretentious attitude. If we were secure about our position at the "top of the food chain" or "natural order," why do we need to defend it so desperately when it is questioned? And why do we attack those who question it? Why do we defend the dominant culture's destruction of both animals and the earth when this destruction is obviously against our own interest in survival?

NATURALISM

The ubiquity of the naturalistic fictions used to defend or promote eating animals, used by religious and secular leaders of all faiths and cultures, is dizzying. But then again, claiming that it is morally acceptable to do something because it comes naturally to us or is grounded in some self-serving conception of the natural order has historically justified some of the most violent and depraved human behaviors, including millennia of institutionalized slavery, rape, pillaging, war, and genocide. Naturalistic fallacies depict nature as some static, simplistic relationship between prey and predator, as portrayed in countless PBS *NATURE* shows. The fact is only 10 percent of all animals are actually carnivorous,[44] and many of these are scavengers who feed on corpses.

Nature is so vast, complex, and elusive, it has always been a profound source of mystery, curiosity, and fascination for us. Perhaps the natural order is beyond human comprehension. But one thing we can say for certain is that just because some custom or routine comes naturally to us certainly does not make it ethical. As author Charles Horn points out in his book *Meat Logic*, "regardless of nature and our own barbaric history, civilization is meant to take us out of the realm of 'survival of the fittest' and 'might makes right' mentalities and to evolve beyond them. Morally speaking, it is time to evolve beyond thinking that our base evolutionary desire gives us the right to exploit, enslave, torture, or kill others. It does not. It is a prejudice."[45]

One form of naturalistic fiction commonly found in popular culture appeals directly to our cravings, convincing us that giving in to our cravings is positively associated with listening and responding to what our bodies really *need*, as if to suggest that the mere fact that we crave or want to eat animals makes it natural or inevitable. We recognize this fictional device when addicts use it to justify smoking cigarettes, abusing alcohol, or gambling compulsively, yet our moral reasoning collapses over our craving for animals, which we claim is not really a vice but instead something to celebrate as natural. Clearly, the darker side of our behavior is as natural as the brighter side, but we only feel compelled to explain why we allow our darker side to eclipse our brighter side. We never feel the need to justify our brighter side because acts of goodness and kindness are accepted on their own merit. "Naturally occurring rape, infanticide, and xenophobia, should help dispel the notion that acting in ways that come 'naturally' automatically fulfills our moral obligations," writes Sherry Colb.[46] Colb argues that we regularly evaluate our own behavior and condemn many instances of naturally occurring conduct. "Indeed, if a particular behavior were sufficiently rare," she explains, "it would suggest that people lack any drive to engage in it, and we would probably need no moral rules forbidding it. From this perspective, it is precisely because both virtue and vice come 'naturally' to us that we must critically consider our activities and choose what to do (and what not to do) on the basis of moral reflection."[47]

Blurring the Distinction between Plants and Animals

"Something must die in order for us to eat. In nature, something always lives by the death of others. The cycle of life and death is a natural process we cannot control and must accept." These are the kinds of justifications and fictions that would have us equate chopping through a head of lettuce with chopping the head off of a bird like a chicken. It is an attempt to bring animal exploitation under the umbrella of "natural processes" much like so many cultures and ages sought to naturalize the institution of slavery or other forms of human exploitation. In an Intelligence Squared debate about the ethics of eating animals, popular sustainable food activist Joel Salatin of Polyface Farms exclaimed, "We're going to have an interesting evening since potatoes have eyes."[48]

Michael Pollan has been instrumental in popularizing the idea that vegans and vegetarians are hypocritical in ignoring the feelings of plants. He does this by intentionally blurring the distinctions between plants and animals and therefore confusing the important ethical considerations we make for sentient beings over nonsentient beings. To his credit, his writings on plant behavior are interesting in their own right,[49] yet the conclusions he draws from them are problematic and sometimes fallacious. One example is Pollan's article published in the *New York Times*, about which Pollan tweeted, "Cool piece on how pea plants communicate with one another, possibly raising some tough issues for vegetarians . . ." One of Pollan's critics, Adam Merberg, who shares a faculty position at UC Berkeley with Pollan, points out in his blog that Pollan's argument for consistency would make sense only if he didn't eat plants—an argument, he writes, "that has nothing to do with whether the person making the argument cares about plants or animals, and everything to do with proving that an argument fails to meet its own standards of consistency."[50]

Aside from the bad logic in these Pollanesque plant defense arguments, there is a common sense reason why we don't hesitate to walk our dogs in the park on the grass (without giving the grass a second thought), yet if someone were to intentionally step on our dog's toes on that walk in the park, we would find this morally objectionable. It would also be within our rights to press criminal charges against the offender. While it is fascinating to learn about new discoveries in plant behavior and even theories about how they might sense harm, the fact remains that the animals we exploit for food clearly and regularly demonstrate that they are highly sentient, emotionally complex individuals who are aware of and value their individual lives. Sentience matters a great deal in this context. Sentient beings have self-awareness and, on the most fundamental level, an interest in avoiding pain, suffering, and death. Plants, not animals, are the foundation of our diet and our survival. Even if plants were discovered to be sentient, raising animals for food requires vastly more plant feed crops than eating plant foods directly from the source. The principle of harm reduction would still logically and ethically compel us to eat plants over animals. While none of us can live completely cruelty-free, the notion that everything we eat, whether of plant or animal origin, has the same moral weight is ethically dishonest and factually inaccurate. So if we can't eliminate our impact on animals, the question then becomes, "How can we minimize it?"

New Age/Progressive Pseudonaturalism

Naturalistic fictions often rely on a strong cultural nostalgia for the past: a simpler, more self-reliant time when our forefathers grew their own food and were closely connected to the land and the plants and animals they raised on it. This idealism ties into a vision of what is "natural" about our relationship with farmed animals: a commodity relationship based on procurer and object. The paleo diet is a testament to what has developed into a movement that ties idealism, naturalism, and traditionalism together in a way that resonates with many. For some notable writers and activists, going "back to the land" means, at least partially, attacking veganism, which rejects animal exploitation on principle and practice. Michael Pollan and Lierre Keith, author of *The Vegetarian Myth*, have both dismissed veganism as a kind of elitist movement composed of urbanites who have no clue about how food is raised, but they conveniently ignore the explosion of vegan sanctuaries that are not only intimately connected with the land but are also often cleaning up farmers' messes by rescuing animals these farmers have abandoned, neglected, or abused. They rescue them not for some ulterior motive but solely out of a desire to help the victims of agriculture.

"That's what they're here for!" is the kind of knee-jerk, thoughtless reaction we have come to expect from some people in response to objections over our use and abuse of farmed animals. Author Barbara Kingsolver lends a kind of pseudointellectual credence to this brand of bigoted "naturalism" in her popular book *Animal, Vegetable, Miracle*. Here she explains that "on our farm, we don't especially enjoy processing our animals, but we do value it as an important ritual for ourselves and any friends adventurous to come and help, because of what we learn from it. We reconnect with the purpose for which these animals were bred. We dispense with all delusions about who put the live in livestock, and who must take it away."[51] Actually, what Kingsolver conveniently dispenses with is morality, any moral consideration for animals or for the fact that their lives might have some meaning to them outside of what she thinks. She does not, however, dispense with the grand delusion—the myth of human supremacy and how we abuse our power over other powerless beings just because we can. She does not reconnect with the essential moral question of dominion and domination over animals, nor does she arrive at some novel explanation of why we should continue this barbaric practice. The attitude she expresses about farmed animals remains much like the group of football fans gathered around a Super Bowl game mindlessly chomping on chicken wings. Kingsolver would only insist that you raise the birds or at least witness their slaughter and dismemberment before you chow down on their wings. So much for the progressive, conscious carnivore.

Hunting, Gathering, and Other Natural Fictions

As already mentioned, arguments from nature often have a deeply entrenched historical footprint, justifying some of the worst, most violent human behavior. Rather than learning from the past, we continue to use the worst of these arguments, like "Animals eat other animals, so why shouldn't we?" and "Do you think that animal wouldn't attack and eat you if given a chance?" and "Do you really think you can stop all carnivores from killing?" Many naturalistic fictions compare carnivorous animals with humans to conclude that eating animals is natural since some other species do it too. Another variation on this plays on the inherent violence in nature as a justification to act violently or make food choices that cause gratuitous violence to nonviolent, enslaved, defenseless animals. It is a dishonest and inaccurate analogy to compare ourselves with the likes of obligate carnivores or even obligate omnivores who kill and eat other animals for reasons of survival while we go about killing animals we've artificially bred for reasons of taste, habit, and economic gain. And even if there were some basis for the comparison, we are in no way obligated to live according to any herd mentality. Quite the contrary, being human means we have a choice. The moral burden of that freedom of choice compels us to spare an innocent animal suffering and death because we *can*—particularly when that choice is so accessible and abundant for the vast majority of us. Or, put another way, in the words of writer Jim Mason, "there are no chains that tie us to human supremacy over an increasingly wounded and bleeding living world."[52]

Hunters and their apologists frequently invoke fictitious natural arguments. Unlike other animals who kill their prey because they are anatomically equipped to do so, human hunters are miserably unequipped for hunting in comparison[53] and instead kill their prey with mechanized lethal weapons to compensate for their physical deficiencies. The fact that true carnivores kill and eat prey animals for reasons of survival is fundamentally different from humans who kill for sport and ego fulfillment. Other animals don't gloat over their trophy kill and post photos of them on Facebook. Even more common than hunters are those who don't hunt at all yet still fancy themselves as predators, even though buying a piece of meat or cheese or a carton of eggs off of the store shelf is about as far from the reality of natural predation as possible. It just means you're paying someone else to bully and kill defenseless baby animals and make them available to you in neatly wrapped packages in the store.

On the other side of this fiction is the idea that our true nature has been subverted by modernity and consumerism. And while we might find the living conditions and behavior of our Paleolithic ancestors rather depraved, paleo-diet proponents claim that their diet still stands as the most natural for us to consume (minus the cannibalism, of course). But is the fact that our ancestors became highly skilled at developing tools of violence and destruction against other beings a part of the human legacy that we really want to celebrate today? While savagely clubbing baby seals to death on ice is part of our natural history, isn't morality natural too? And doesn't the arc of recent times lean toward justice, as Martin Luther King Jr. famously said, and compel us to reject our last great bastion of prejudice against species, species who share our fundamental capacity for suffering? Human civilizations have used elaborate rituals around the killing of animals for food as a form of repentance and absolution of guilt for causing them suffering and loss of life, even when they believed it was necessary.

To illustrate this point, consider your reaction to the sight of a lion tearing apart a zebra as she cries out in anguish. For many it will be disgust or pity or horror. In any case, we hope that the zebra suffered as little as possible, but we still can't get over what a horrible way this would be to die. And how about the sight of a dead animal on the side of the road or even a living cow grazing on a pasture? In any of these cases, do you start drooling at the mouth and work up an appetite? Where is our hunter-gatherer instinct at these moments of witnessing either violent deaths or happy living animals? Our reactions are very revealing about the core of our moral nature; namely, our aversion to unnecessary suffering. When it comes to the animal products we regularly consume, most people find it too painful to face the reality of the animal's experience on farms and slaughterhouses. We are cavalier about not feeling remorse for animals who were "treated humanely" to feed our guts yet would never do to baby animals what we pay desensitized workers to do to them.

The assertion that we are predisposed to eating animals by our very nature has led to a proliferation of scientific research and philosophical inquiry, the result of which is humbling and sometimes altogether irrelevant. Much has been written and debated about other animals and their place in our moral community. Some researchers argue that we are fundamentally moral beings and that morality is what makes us uniquely human. Much research has been done about how empathy for and interest in animals develops in children.[54] Still others, like author and psychologist Jeff Masson, seek to understand why we are so uniquely violent as a species. "They [other animals] rarely kill their own," Masson points out in the trailer for his book *Beasts: What Animals Can Teach Us About the Origins of Good and Evil*.[55] "In the 20th century alone humans have slaughtered over 200 million of our own kind. Why are we so different?" In his innovative book *The Moral Lives of Animals*, animal behaviorist Dale Peterson seeks to show how social and moral behavior in the species he has studied is the antecedent for human morality as it came to be articulated in the Ten Commandments and the New Testament. And yet, regardless of what approach resonates with us, the fact remains that if animals matter to us, even only marginally, then we don't violate their most basic right to life and liberty when we can easily avoid it. If we believe that part of what makes us uniquely human is our moral compass, then perhaps what is *natural* for us to eat is what causes us the least remorse; that is, doing the least harm, especially when we become aware of the impact of our food choices, especially when we face an abundance of alternatives from which to choose.

Naturally Unsustainable

In response to growing consumer disenchantment with the environmental nightmare of so-called factory farms, a new brand of farmers has emerged to promote a more "sustainable" form of raising animals. *Grass-fed beef. Free-range chickens. Pasture-raised pork.* The animals they raise, they claim, are allowed to express their natural behaviors, raised in natural environments, fed a natural diet, and even provide benefits back to the environment. But comparing against the worst-case scenario will always make a bad scenario look better. Just because something is better doesn't mean it's sustainable or natural. When compared to a plant-based diet, any kind of animal-based diet is miserably unsustainable.[56] And even if it were true that eating animals had a lower environmental impact over eating plants, would that in itself make exploiting and killing animals for food ethical or natural? If one could demonstrate that sweatshops had a lower environmental impact than other, less exploitative forms of garment production, would that factor alone make it ethical to exploit workers? Obviously not. Fortunately, we don't need to contemplate such an ethical dilemma in the case of eating animals since there is an overwhelming amount of evidence showing the staggering environmental impact of animal agriculture.[57] Is it natural that a single species artificially breeds and kills sixty billion land animals and another trillion marine animals every year? The bottom line is that we eat all of these animals out of convenience, habit, tradition, palate pleasure, and profit. Our demand for animal products supports a $154.8 billion meat industry that profits from the abject and needless suffering of some ten billion animals annually in the US alone.[58]

Promoting the Unnatural as Natural

Some naturalistic fictions rely on the public's ignorance about farmed animals and the practices of modern agriculture. For example, it takes a tremendous amount of fictional prowess to sustain the idea that cow's milk is necessary and natural for our health. The result is a society that regards drinking human mother's breast milk as disgusting, but gives no thought to why they regularly consume the milk of another species—and all of the other dairy products derived from the milk, believing that cow's milk is not just edible but indispensable. In one of the Milk Mustache ads, a mother holds her two infants, suggesting that drinking cow's milk is as natural as breastfeeding your own babies. The dairy industry has most people believing that cow's milk, and the cheese, yogurt, butter, ice cream, and other products derived from it, are natural for us to consume. But if these products are indeed so natural, then why is dairy farming based on so many extremely unnatural practices?

More specifically, what's natural about so-called artificial insemination? Nearly 80 percent of dairy cows in the United States are forcibly impregnated repeatedly in a crude procedure that involves workers inserting one arm all the way up a cow's rectum to optimally position her cervix, while using the other hand to insert an "AI [artificial insemination] gun" full of semen into her vagina.[59] Rectal violation plays no part in natural bovine copulation. For that matter, what's natural about controlling the reproduction of other animals?

What's natural about collecting semen from bulls by ejaculating them using either an artificial vagina or an instrument called an electro-ejaculator? With the first method, a steer is usually restrained and used as a "teaser" animal to be mounted. The bull is tethered and controlled with a nose ring. After the bull mounts the steer and attempts penetration, his exposed penis is grabbed by a worker and diverted to a long plastic sleeve, or "artificial vagina," held in the worker's other hand. With electro-ejaculation, an anal probe is inserted into the bull's rectum and electric shock applied to the muscles that control ejaculation.

What's natural about an animal's udders being hooked up to mechanized milking that sucks milk out of her mammary glands? What's natural about biologically manipulating cows to produce up to twelve times more milk than their bodies were designed for?[60] According to John Webster, professor emeritus of animal husbandry at Bristol University, "the amount of work done by the dairy cow in peak lactation is immense. To achieve a comparable high work rate, a human would have to jog for about 6 hours a day, every day."[61] What's natural about dairy cow diseases resulting from confinement and overproduction of milk, such as lameness and mastitis, the two most common reasons reported for early death or slaughter of dairy cows?[62] What's natural about artificially breeding millions of cows only to slaughter them at a fraction of their natural lifespan, when their milk production declines? In fact, more than three million young dairy cows are slaughtered each year—about one-third of the entire US dairy herd—and processed into ground beef.[63]

What's natural about permanently removing calves from their mothers at birth? Whether on factory farms or small farms, separation of cows and their calves is a fundamental practice of dairy farming. But cows are devoted mothers, and researchers find that merely five minutes of contact between a cow and her newborn calf is sufficient for the formation of a strong maternal bond.[64] Cows used for dairy search for their stolen calves and often call for them for days. What's natural about forcing newborn calves to live in isolated hutches for their first months of life, confined without any maternal nurturing, or killing them immediately if they are unmarketable as veal? Like their brothers raised for veal, female calves used for dairy are also typically raised in lonely stalls or hutches. What's natural about feeding calves raised for veal a diet that makes them anemic and malnourished, often unable to walk or even stand when loaded for transport to slaughter?[65] What's natural about inserting a spiked nose ring into a calf's nose to prevent him from suckling on his mother's udders? This is a common technique on the few small farms where calves are permitted to stay with their mothers for more than a few days. What's natural about humans consuming—into adulthood—the milk of another species exclusively formulated and intended for the animal's own babies, and when even that animal's own offspring are weaned off of their mother's milk by the first year of age? What's natural about drinking dairy milk when most of the global population can't even digest or tolerate it? What's natural about forcing children to consume something their bodies were never designed for, a fluid consistently linked with childhood asthma, allergies, ear infections, rashes, and juvenile diabetes?[66]

NECESSITY

The first major form of the necessity fiction is based on the idea that we kill animals out of a need to feed ourselves. Television series like PBS's *NATURE*, BBC and Discovery Channel's *Human Planet*, and many series on the National Geographic Channel portray indigenous people as hunting and killing animals out of necessity yet with deep remorse, always honoring the animal for their "sacrifice" with some kind of gratitude ritual. Contrary to popular belief, animals have not been systematically used and abused and killed throughout history for reasons of necessity alone, but for a variety of other unnecessary reasons as well, like status, sport, fashion, and ritual. Indeed, hunting in most cultures had become a measure of masculinity, bravery, and skill. A prime example of the human legacy of animal exploitation is the wild turkey, who is known to have lived some ten million years ago[67] and was first "domesticated" around 800 BC by Native Americans in south-central Mexico, primarily for fashion. Turkey feathers, not turkey flesh, was what they were after.[68] Prior to this assault on wild turkeys, these birds lived without human interference for millennia.[69] In their article entitled "Native Americans First Tamed Turkeys 2,000 Years Ago," Discovery Communications frames this history euphemistically, suggesting that we've done these animals some kind of favor rather than destroying their way of life as free beings by systematically capturing, confining, and killing them for their feathers. In ancient Egypt, fully conscious calves and other animals were ritually slaughtered and used as burial offerings as a symbol of the deceased person's status.

The fictional device of necessity is often weaved in with other fictional devices—like tradition, evolution, and biology—in an effort to build the case for exploiting and eating animals. Making the case for necessity is enormously important to animal agriculture and their defenders and apologists, since, if actually true, necessity would be the one credible defense for the immense suffering we cause billions of farmed animals annually.

Nutrition as Necessity
The second major form of the necessity fiction is based on the idea that we cannot get all the nutrients we need from plants. Tied to this is the misconception of what the term omnivore actually means: an animal who is able to obtain his nutrients from either plant or

animal origin. As humans, we can't live without plants or we would likely die, but we can easily live without animal products. Clinging to the belief that eating animals is a biological necessity is a fiercely protected fiction, since without necessity, our only valid reason for causing animals suffering vanishes. As a result, the most vociferous attacks and fearmongering over the plant-based diet come from those institutions that have the most to lose from debunking the necessity of consuming animal products. In sectors like milk where sales of plant-based milks have significantly contributed to a decline in cow's milk sales,[70] we've seen the dairy industry react with marketing campaigns appealing to our fear of not getting enough calcium and protein and/or appealing to our desire for authenticity by positioning cow's milk as the "real thing" and plant milks as fakes or imitators. The REAL Dairy logo that the dairy industry launched four decades ago continues to function as the industry's seal of authenticity. Their 2014 video called "Don't be Fooled by the Imitators" features a squatty little professor who tells us, "It's not real dairy if it's made with a bean, a seed, a nut, or a weed."[71] The irony of course is that the cow they use to produce all that milk for them has a natural diet of "weeds" from which she obtains all the calcium and other nutrients she needs to build those large and sturdy bones and provide her calves with nutritious baby formula over the course of an entire year of nursing.

And it's not just the cow's natural behavior that exposes the claims of the dairy industry as fictional. Several of the world's leading health authorities, including the Academy of Nutrition and Dietetics (formerly known as the American Dietetic Association), also defy all the fear- and necessity-based fictions out there with official statements affirming that "appropriately planned vegetarian diets, including total vegetarian or vegan diets, are healthful, nutritionally adequate, and may provide health benefits in the prevention and treatment of certain diseases. Well-planned vegetarian diets are appropriate for individuals during all stages of the life cycle, including pregnancy, lactation, infancy, childhood, and adolescence, and for athletes."[72] Yet, even if we lacked the abundance of studies affirming the benefits of a plant-based diet, it would be impossible to ignore the some seven hundred million vegetarians who generally thrive from a diet of little to no animal products. And those are just the self-professed vegetarians. Billions of others actually consume a mostly-plant diet simply out of economic necessity and with dramatically lower incidences of chronic Western diseases that afflict the most affluent and indulgent eaters on our planet.

Feeding the World

When not justifying animal consumption for historical or health reasons, the necessity fiction manifests in its third major form as the "feeding the world" mantra, in which animal agriculture positions itself as heroically coming to the rescue of the world's hungry. But is this agenda really that altruistic? And even if it were, at what cost? In the process of feeding the affluent world with animal flesh and secretions, they are also contributing to unprecedented rates of chronic disease, climate and environmental crises, one of the great mass extinctions of species, and actually exacerbating world hunger and political and economic instability in certain regions of the world. According the United Nations World Food Programme, 795 million people on the planet don't have enough to eat to lead a healthy, active life,[73] not even basic staple grains, but animal agriculture still manages to find plenty of grains to feed some sixty billion artificially bred farmed animals. So long as we allow the global food industry to prioritize the marketing of the animal-focused Western diet as a sign of social mobility and affluence throughout the world, "feeding the world" will mean nothing more than a hollow brand message that conceals the industry's real agenda of expanding lucrative export markets for animal products at the expense of the world's neediest and the environment.

Promoting Animal Consumption as Social Justice

The fourth major form of the necessity fiction is expressed through the idea that a "greater good" is served by exploiting animals; in this case, feeding hungry humans. One of the leading nonprofit hunger relief organizations, Feeding America, sponsored a campaign in collaboration with SuperValu Food Stores and the Dairy Council with the campaign message "Don't let him go without milk." The campaign posters were plastered on the windows of SuperValu stores and cash register monitors showing a young African American boy jumping in midair as if splashing into a puddle of milk. The campaign goes beyond just falsely suggesting that milk is necessary for human health; it asserts that depriving children of cow's milk is an injustice comparable to letting them go hungry. This is a false dilemma. For example, a glass of fortified soy milk (or any other fortified plant-based milk) can provide the nutrients we get from a glass of fortified cow's milk and without supporting animal exploitation and violence, without supporting the war on wildlife,[74] without the need to feed nutritious plant crops to dairy cows that could otherwise feed hungry people, without the devastating environmental impact, and without all of the heavy metals, pesticides, industrial pollutants (like dioxins and PCBs), hormones, growth factors, blood cells, and other unhealthy contaminants concentrated in cow's milk. The fact that the campaign is marketed to inner-city, lower-income youth makes it even more insidious since this demographic has the least access to solid information on nutrition and nutritious food options. Instead their neighborhoods are inundated with the shiny, new fast food establishments of every popular brand.

Another major vehicle for promoting animal exploitation and consumption as "social justice" comes from the animal gifting industry. Organizations like World Vision, Heifer International, and Oxfam build their nonprofit brands on the basis of the necessity fiction by promoting a Western diet and dominionist ideology as a solution to world hunger in areas of the world where our Western, Christian ideals can cause more harm than good. According to Heifer legend, Ohio farmer Dan West had the idea for giving cows to the poor as a Christian aid worker rationing milk to refugee children in the late 1930s. The charity, first called Heifers for

Relief, was incorporated in 1944 and sent its first shipment of seventeen heifers to Puerto Rico. The first animals were lactating cows named Faith, Hope, and Charity.[75] In Heifer's donor appeal video, narrator Alton Brown stresses the good, old-fashioned virtues of teaching people self-reliance over just giving them a handout, and he addresses what must be a common objection to gifting animals instead of modern farm equipment that could more efficiently do the work that animals once did. "An animal is a much better engine [than a tractor]; you turn it on. It gives you milk or wool or eggs," says Brown, promoting the fiction that animals just magically produce product for us without cost, human labor, or resources.[76] To soften this image of animals as machines, woven throughout the video and the elaborate print catalogs are frequent photos of adorable baby animals in the arms of children of varied ethnicities. But Dawn Moncrief, president of the hunger relief and animal advocacy nonprofit A Well Fed World, argues that Heifer's mission of promoting food justice and hunger relief through an increased reliance on farmed animals is problematic on several levels. In parts of the world where natural resources are critically scarce and/or ravaged by drought, desertification, and deforestation, "sustainable plant crops that actually provide better nutrition and more income are often overlooked."[77] Also, many of those who receive farmed animals through these programs "struggle to provide even the most basic care to the animals they receive." In some cases, it makes a bad situation even worse. "Having another mouth to feed," says Moncrief, "can significantly add to a family's burden and animals frequently suffer from neglect, malnutrition, dehydration, lack of veterinary care, and lack of shelter from temperature extremes."[78]

Euphemism

Euphemism as a fictional device—and language as a general matter—are essential tools for crafting the stories and messages from animal agriculture. Take, for example, the powerful words *animal husbandry*, which frame farmers as the benevolent masters and protectors of other animals. The animal's very existence is defined by serving us, and in return for this honor, she willingly gives us her milk, eggs, babies, body, and ultimately her very life when she outlives her usefulness to us. The language we carefully select affirms that the relationship is symbiotic or mutually beneficial. We never say we *take* from her. *Giving* is positively associated with sacrifice and altruism, so here we have an example of euphemism motivated by human ambition and built upon anthropomorphism (the "altruistic" cow sacrificing her milk for us). On the other hand, *taking* is negatively associated with stealing what doesn't belong to you. So we are careful to never characterize ourselves as *takers*. Animal agriculture has created a strategic vocabulary of euphemisms intended to make us feel good, or at least better, about imposing needless suffering on animals for food.

"A is for Animal: The Lexicon of Animal Use" is author Joel Marks's useful guide to many of the most common terms intended "to maintain their mastery or prerogatives over other animals." Marks feels so strongly about the power of words in this context, he claims that "putting on display the verbal menagerie in animal agriculture, animal experimentation, and the rest of the industries and institutions that use nonhuman animals, could go a long way toward eliminating these enterprises, since they are built as much on equivocation as on exploitation."[79] Marks covers some unlikely words that most people would not consider in an evaluation of euphemisms, like the word *animal* itself, explaining that "the federal government's primary legislation governing animal welfare does not recognize the vast majority of animals used for food, research, and sport, nor under the jurisdiction of wilderness managers, as animals. The primary intended beneficiaries of the Animal Welfare Act were probably the animals that Americans view as pets."[80] Marks's work seems to build upon the classic work of Joan Dunayer, who may have been the first to write a comprehensive book about language and the oppression of other animals.[81]

"Domestication"

Most of us are conditioned by the farming industry to believe that animals have to be happy to produce for farmers. "If farmers didn't take good care of their animals, they wouldn't produce for them." Statements like this coming from farmers themselves reveal how we've deluded ourselves into believing that farmed animals desire the fate to which we've doomed them rather than desire the lives of free beings, free in mobility but also in intention, which can only derive from minds that express a complex range of interests and desires. What we call domestication is nothing short of the wholesale capture, confinement, breeding, and commodification of wild animals which began some ten thousand years ago. In his book *An Unnatural Order*, Jim Mason explains that the "control and manipulation of animals — their numbers, sizes, and shapes — became almost an obsession in herding cultures. In time, control came to be valued in and of itself. It was the way of the Good Shepherd, a patriarchal model for the guilt-free exploitation of animals and natural processes."[82] And even though most of modern civilization has moved far from the lifestyle of herding cultures, we still seem to attach an almost sacred, symbolic value to this tradition that brands seek to awaken in us. "Our culture today," writes Will Tuttle, "for all its technical gadgetry, is still at its core a herding culture that defines itself and everyone in it by the pervasive practice of enslaving animals for food and products."[83] Mason describes how the Good Shepherd of domestication, the deified tamer of wild beasts, became embedded into the world's major religions as "generations of prophets, philosophers, poets, and preachers filled out, refined, and updated the model," while "some went down in history as the great men of our civilization."[84] Today, celebrity farmers the likes of Joel Salatin, a key protagonist in the documentary *Food Inc.*, have become the modern-day Good Shepherds, building their brands around a vision of a sustainable future built upon an ancient legacy of animal oppression that is, in truth, far less sustainable than growing plant foods.

"Artificial Insemination"

To appreciate how euphemistic *artificial insemination* is when referring to the forced and systematic breeding practices of farmed animals, we must first consider what it means in the case of human beings. For starters, artificial insemination in female humans is elective, not forced upon them. Next, artificial insemination is seen as a hopeful solution, a *good* technology that could actually help a couple achieve their lifelong dream of having a family. And finally, insemination is a short, relatively painless procedure that many women describe as being similar to a Pap smear. But in dairy cows, dairy goats, turkeys, and other farmed animals, the procedure is none of these things. For one thing, it causes clear signs of emotional distress and physical pain.[85] What's worse, the procedures that involve shooting semen into the vagina of female animals and (rectal penetration in cows) are crude, invasive, and often performed by farm workers who have little or no veterinary experience. AI, as it is called in the industry, is done repeatedly until it is certain that the animal becomes pregnant. After repeated birthing, she becomes "spent" and therefore an economic liability to farmers who then send her to slaughter. All of this is done without the animal understanding why she is being violated or why her offspring are being taken from her. Using *artificial insemination* to refer to this cruel and perverse assault on farmed animals is a classic example of how euphemisms in animal agriculture function to mask a terrible truth.

"Heritage Breeds" and "Livestock Conservation"

Bison, the icon of American culture, which was once hunted to near extinction, has now been bred for one of the trendiest new flesh products. Broken Wagon Bison Farm outside of Chicago offers visitors a chance to pet and feed gentle and friendly bison and then visit their store where they can stock up on bison flesh products and fashion apparel made from their skins and bones. The whole experience, from the petting zoo to the retail store, is carefully branded and packaged using patriotic language and visuals, such as portraits of Native Americans thanking bison and nostalgic landscapes of bison roaming freely on the range—all in an effort to conceal the violence and killing at the core of the enterprise. The overall sentiment of the experience is embodied in the idea of conservation: the idea that they're doing the bison a favor by bringing their population back, even if only to use and slaughter their babies while their flesh is still nice and tender.

Broken Wagon Bison Farm is just one of many examples of a larger effort by the sustainable/humane food movement to popularize such euphemisms as *heritage breed*, which refers to livestock breeds that are allegedly more natural, traditional, and better suited to their environment. The Livestock Conservancy, a leading voice in the so-called livestock conservation movement, defines *heritage* as "traditional livestock breeds that were raised by our forefathers. . . . breeds of a bygone era," and warns us that "heritage animals once roamed the pastures of America's pastoral landscape, but today these breeds are in danger of extinction."[86] This statement suggests that humankind did Mother Nature a favor by domesticating certain indigenous species and by introducing invasive species to her ecosystems, as if nothing existed (or at least nothing worth conserving) before our intervention, as if no species were harmed or hunted to extinction in the process of converting and maintaining once pristine ecosystems into farmland. In reality, farmers wreaked havoc on ecosystems and systematically killed off other animals that posed a threat or nuisance to their livestock investments. And the process continues today, particularly on so-called pasture-based or free-range farms, which require more land use and more confrontations with indigenous species.

Even the Livestock Conservancy admits that *heritage* is "largely a term of art and not science."[87] But is this really art or just another euphemism strategically branded for an affluent and highly lucrative niche market, which the conservancy claims is needed "to secure the term in the food and agricultural marketplaces so that it becomes a term that consumers can rely upon"?[88] In other words, the motivation is about manipulating consumer perceptions, not conservation. And the brand is built upon a story about animal "martyrs" who we must kill and eat in order to ultimately save from extinction: "Most heritage breeds are also endangered breeds, so by defining Heritage it allows for the reintroduction of these breeds to the marketplace as the cultural and culinary treasures that they are."[89]

By calling this livestock conservation, farmers who buy heritage-breed animals are suddenly elevated and likened to the altruistic intentions of true species conservationists, who are driven by their passion for protecting those species rather than making a living off of exploiting them. A *livestock conservationist*, on the other hand, can breed and raise animals for the sole purpose of slaughtering them in their infancy or adolescence—at a fraction of their natural lifespan—to make a living off of selling their carcasses as "culinary treasures" and call himself a conservationist. In any other context, conservation means the opposite; it means helping the members of a species to live out their natural lifespan and encouraging them to mate and have natural families to increase their population and then to release them into the natural world. The goal is not to turn them into "culinary treasures" for our own selfish enjoyment, but to instead preserve their heritage because we recognize their intrinsic value. If we were to apply the logic of livestock conservation to other animals, it would mean that poaching, hunting, killing, and eating them, rather than actually protecting them from human destruction, would be not just acceptable but worthy of the term *conservation*.

As for the issue of extinction, animals we have intensively bred and transformed through centuries of domination never existed in the natural world to begin with, so it is impossible for them to go extinct. Only animals that exist in the natural world, not domesticated versions of animals we exploit for our own purposes, are subject to extinction. In many cases, we've already hunted their natural ancestors to extinction long ago. But even if one insists that it would be a great tragedy for these so-called heritage breeds to disappear, since when is it logical that breeding them into this world means we must also kill and eat their infant bodies too? It seems that our fear of farmed-animal extinction is more about the conservation of our ego, that these animals are symbolic as our own proud creation, a testament to our superiority and ingenuity.

The fictional premise that livestock conservation plays a vital ecological role in the restoration of ecosystems has not gone completely unchallenged. According to environmental author Will Anderson, this premise is false. Anderson argues that "restoring prairie ecosystems does not require livestock; conservation biologists can and should employ native species instead."[90] He goes on to say that

> ecosystems do not need billions of domesticated livestock from invasive species to achieve *stimulated* plant communities; we can accomplish magnitudes of recovery more if conservation biologists introduce native species in tandem with the end of animal agriculture. As it dies, ecosystems will thrive. Conservation biologists will need generations before plant and animal communities regain at least some relationships that are essential to the ecosystems. Grazing cattle will be replaced by the original inhabitants, the bison, antelope, deer, tallgrass and shortgrass, prairie chickens, and ground squirrels. Highlands and lowlands, forests and plains, all should be rid of the pox that livestock represent.[91]

Moreover, animal agriculture posing as a conservation effort is a fiction. It's a business of making money on the exploited and then slaughtered bodies of other animals. What could be the benefit to any human or nonhuman animal to be brought into this world under such circumstances? If you knew your life would be defined by enslavement, mutilations, sexual violation, reproductive control, the theft of your offspring, and a violent slaughterhouse end in your youth, what would be the advantage of being born? Knowing the horrors of human tyranny?

The Word *Meat*

Everyone uses the word *meat*, even those who care passionately about animals. But we rarely consider the meaning behind the word. To illustrate this, Free from Harm created a Facebook meme showing one of its beautiful rescued ducks, Ginger, next to an image of a pathetic, disfigured, and defeathered smoked Pekin duck hung by his wings with his head and long bill cowering downward in a storefront window. The tagline reads " 'Meat' is a beautiful someone brutalized into no one." *Meat* is the word our culture conditions us to use in place of *animal*. *Meat* is the objectification of a someone who had a mind equipped for functioning in a complex natural environment: finding the right mate, building shelters, giving birth, finding and storing food for the family, raising and educating young, negotiating and communicating with others in large social groups, learning from past events and anticipating future events, experiencing and expressing likes, dislikes, pains, pleasures, loves, and losses.

But we also use the word *meat* to denigrate some of our own kind as well, such as when we refer to someone as a "piece of meat," a piece of property to be controlled, trafficked, and exploited for someone else's gain or pleasure. Author Carol Adams presents a pioneering analysis of this idea in her groundbreaking book *The Sexual Politics of Meat*. "Meat is king; the noun describing meat is a noun denoting male power," writes Adams. "Since women have been made subsidiary in a male-dominated, meat-eating world, so has our food. The foods associated with second-class citizens are considered to be second-class proteins. Just as it is thought a woman cannot make it on her own, so we think that vegetables cannot make a meal on their own."[92]

A number of other euphemisms have become so enshrined in popular culture today that they are used without even thinking about their immense power in reinforcing our skewed perception of farmed animals. *Harvesting* refers to the slaughter of animals, as if to suggest that the violent killing of animals is synonymous with pulling root vegetables out of the soil. *Processing* is a more clinical and cleaner euphemism for describing the bloody and messy reality of slaughter, which also employs the objectification fictional device described earlier in this chapter, reinforcing the fiction that animals are just objects, like dough balls processed into dinner rolls.

Euthanasia is a word that has been deceptively applied to the killing of healthy infant or adolescent-age animals who want to live, rather than its original meaning, which refers to someone who has given his consent to take his life as an alternative to prolonging the suffering of a terminal illness. According to Merriam-Webster's online dictionary, euthanasia is "the act or practice of killing someone who is very sick or injured in order to prevent any more suffering."[93] Consent is a vital factor, perhaps even the deciding factor, between mercy killing and murder. And animals cannot give their consent to be killed or, for that matter, used in any way against their will. Therefore applying the term *euthanasia* in the context of killing animals who indicate their desire to stay alive is a dishonest attempt to put a humane face on the act of taking an animal's life only to satisfy the pleasure we derive from eating their flesh or secretions.

Chapter 4:

Humane-washing: Sealing the Foundation

As more people become aware of so-called factory farming, the humane movement has emerged as animal agriculture's key strategy to intercept the conversation and deflect it away from veganism and retain consumers by using a sophisticated set of marketing fictions we collectively call humane-washing. The rhetoric often relies on a classic tale of good and evil, quite literally the Good Shepherd or renegade antiestablishment farmer against the power-hungry, greedy agribusiness industry. Yet, as author Hope Bohanec points out in her article "The Humane Hoax," "The disheartening truth is that . . . the similarities far outweigh the differences. Most of the other horrors a farmed animal endures in animal agriculture still apply to any of these alternative labels."[94] And where, you might ask, do these reassuring labels come from?

AMERICAN HUMANE CERTIFIED

Major certifications programs like American Humane Certified have provided the animal exploitation industries with the official seal of approval that they need from respected, independent organizations to gain widespread public trust. One of the largest and most visible of these organizations is the American Humane Association. Foster Farms, which claims to be the "West Coast leader in antibiotic and organic chicken," created a slick promotional video for the sole purpose of promoting its American Humane certification, which is featured prominently on its website. Charles Consiglia, manager of veterinarian services at Foster Farms, readily admits in the video that "what American Humane is providing is basically a trusted validation for how we are raising these birds."[95] So what does the certification actually mean to the birds? Rich Musselman, field operations manager at AHA, explains in the video, "Our [AHA] audit is built around the five freedoms . . . the freedom from hunger and thirst, freedom from discomfort, freedom from pain and injury, freedom to express natural behaviors, and freedom from fear and distress."[96]

In stark contrast to Musselman's pious performance in this promotional video, another Foster Farms commercial portrays happy chicken puppet characters that are just ecstatic about the AHA humane certification program. The trivialization fantasy here is akin to the Tyson Foods commercial depicting chickens in front of a dressing table and mirror, as if getting dolled up to go out on the town. In both cases, humor and trivialization are powerful fictional devices used to mask the violence and oppression at the core of their business. The Foster Farms commercial became such a public relations fiasco that Peninsula Humane Society & SPCA president Ken White publicly slammed the AHA in the *Huffington Post*, writing, "My issue here is about messaging which reduces live animals to talking fools so desperate to be eaten that they adopt slapstick antics to fool us into thinking they were raised by this manufacturer rather than that manufacturer. And I am offended that an organization with the word *humane* in its name would lend that name to this effort."[97] The commercial is no longer available on YouTube.

Aside from the creepy juxtaposition of chickens destined for slaughter represented as cartoon characters that appeal to children, and aside from the underlying premise of claiming that it is humane to kill animals we have no need to eat, what's really striking is just how meaningless the AHA's "five freedoms" are in practice. Take, for example, the "freedom from hunger and thirst." It is rare that a farm intentionally starves or dehydrates animals they have a vested financial interest in raising and fattening up to reach market weight (with the exception of perhaps forced molting in the egg industry). Broiler chickens are permitted to do little more than eat in their short lives so that they will grow to market weight as quickly as possible. They are confined to crowded spaces intentionally, getting little or no exercise and opportunity to burn calories.

The remaining freedoms focus mainly on freedom from pain, stress, discomfort, fear, and injury and disease. How is it that the AHA can even claim to know, much less monitor on an individual level, what each chicken on each farm it certifies is experiencing, feeling, or thinking? Chickens are individuals, with individual personalities, likes, and dislikes. On sanctuaries, one chicken delights at the sight of a new visitor and eagerly approaches him with great curiosity, while another seeks a hiding place. A different visitor can elicit a completely different response from the same chicken. This indicates that they perceive us as individuals and respond accordingly. As for freedom from injuries and disease, poultry farms perform "flock management," which means they treat the entire flock with the same procedures and drugs in the hopes of reducing disease, casualties, and thus economic losses. They do not provide individualized care by a veterinarian in the hopes of extending and improving the quality of their lives. This would be cost prohibitive for birds that have little market value and are killed within weeks of their birth.

It would be difficult to find a more cynical or deceptive form of humane-washing propaganda than this Foster Farms commercial suggesting that animals have some kind of perverse suicidal death wish. More conventional humane-washing from the meat industry is typically less contrived and more directly delivering the message "We raise happy animals, so please buy our products with a clear conscience." The Foster Farms–AHA collaboration represents a whole new level of appealing to the hearts and minds of consumers who care about animals and desperately want to believe in the humane myth. Moreover, the notion that an individual is "free" from certain emotional states in an environment in which they are enslaved, confined, and killed in their infancy is a myth that can only be explained by the logic of meat-industry storytelling, which seeks to turn reality on its head by portraying the victim as happy to be victimized.

But Foster Farm's fictional props of happy birds raised organically and humanely would soon be shattered. In 2013, as the largest salmonella outbreak in history was unfolding, Foster Farms acquired AHA certification even though conditions at Foster Farms were virtually identical to every other major chicken farm. Consequently, today every package of Foster Farms chicken bears the AHA label. Then, in June 2015, footage from a major undercover investigation at Foster Farms was released by Mercy for Animals depicting a world of abject misery for baby birds. The birds in the investigation are the same used throughout the poultry industry: Cornish rock chickens engineered and bred to grow so large and so fast they commonly suffer from painful lameness and heart and other organ failure even before they reach slaughter weight at six weeks old. In the footage, slaughterhouse workers showed sadistic pleasure in torturing these birds, violently slamming them into metal leg shackles, punching and throwing them around, and ripping feathers out of them for pleasure. According to Mercy for Animals, "once shackled, the birds are dragged through an electrified vat of water meant to paralyze them, but not necessarily render them unconscious. This means that many chickens are still completely conscious and able to feel pain when their throats are cut open. Those who miss the kill blade because they were hung improperly by careless workers are often scalded alive in the hot feather-removal tanks. . . . unconscionable cruelty and violence are standard practice at Foster Farms and other 'American Humane Certified' factory farms."[98] Then later that same year, a Compassion Over Killing investigator released footage from a Foster Farms turkey hatchery in Fresno, California, for which CNN aired an in-depth exclusive report. At this facility, 4.5 million turkey poults are born into a living hell every year, roughly handled by machines that operate at extreme speeds and that mutilate their beaks and toes. Sick, injured, or weak birds not fit for sale are tossed aside and either gassed to death or ground up alive by meat grinders.

BEYOND THE HUMANE CERTIFICATIONS

"Okay, so the major certification programs like AHA are a scam, but surely there must be some alternatives that actually have some integrity?" This is the inevitable question from those still groping for some shred of integrity in animal agriculture. "It can't be all bad. We couldn't have been wrong all of this time, could we?" Those who grapple with such questions are on the threshold of discovering the depths of depravity and dishonesty in the humane movement.

But let's entertain the questions by considering what many might consider a best-case scenario, the case of Riverford's Organic Chickens,[99] a small, independent farm in Ireland that appears, at least on the surface, to fulfill our utopian Old McDonald's Farm fantasy. What do the highest standards of welfare actually mean to the animals? By allowing his chickens to live five weeks longer than those raised on factory farms and by allowing them a few hours a day to forage on a pasture, the farmer interviewed in Riverford's promotional video claims that he raises "happy chickens." He is practically deified by enthusiastic YouTube followers who are naively seduced into believing that chickens are simpleminded animals who can actually live fulfilling lives if only we allow them to be raised on a bucolic-looking family farm by a nice-looking, smiley-faced farmer. But the sanitized slice of reality presented here could not be more staged and shallow.

The farmer gently and affectionately holds one of his beautiful weeks-old chickens, as he reassures us that "they have a great life." What the video does not show us is how he betrays the trust he has gained from these birds by violently ending their lives while still in their infancy. He does not show us the fear, stress, and screams they express when caught by human hands and carried upside down by their feet. He does not show how they will be stuffed into crates and loaded onto transport trucks. He does not show how they will endure a grueling transport without food or water or protection from the elements. And even if he spares them the miseries of transport, he does not show how he will stuff them, head first and kicking and screaming, down kill cones to have their necks pulled through the opening at the bottom. He does not show how they will have their necks, full of a multitude of sensitive pain receptors, slashed with a knife and how their bodies will thrash in the cone in agony for up to eight minutes while the blood drains from their bodies and out of their necks and mouths, as they slowly lose consciousness. He does not show how they will then be dumped in a scalding tank and then thrown into a defeathering machine where their pitiful corpses will be repeatedly pummeled by large iron "claws" designed to tear all of their feathers from their body. He does not show where his "breeding stock" comes from, the same laboratories and breeding factories where biologically engineered birds are selectively bred and sold to factory farms, where the cruelest practices ever developed in animal agriculture are inflicted on billions of birds day in and day out. He does not explain the abhorrent health issues inherent in the biological manipulation of their bodies forcing them to grow into freakishly large, adult-size bodies in a mere forty-two days, while still in their infancy.

He excludes all of the above fundamental truths that are undeniably central to his business of raising happy-meat chickens because telling the whole truth would sabotage his happy-meat fantasy. The whole truth would terrify almost any potential happy-meat consumer who wants to believe in the fantasy world he props up just for them. His humane-washed reality becomes the basis for the self-deception upon which they base their food choices.

THE CASE OF TEMPLE GRANDIN

Temple Grandin, a professor of animal science at Colorado State University, is a key figure of the humane movement. The 2010 HBO film of the same name portrays Grandin as a kind of "Mother Teresa" of farmed animals, working inside the animal industrial complex to lessen the suffering of animals by way of her trademark invention she proudly refers to as "the stairway to heaven," where adolescent cows are led, more calmly, to their violent deaths. The film introduced Grandin to a wide audience who had never heard of her before, catapulting her career into popular culture. In a short time, she became somewhat of a media icon and her name became synonymous with the humane movement, so much so that even animal advocacy organizations like the Humane Society of the United States and Mercy for Animals began to quote her as an expert source in their farm investigatory work. The film also highlights her ability to succeed in the male-dominated agricultural industry as a woman and as an autistic person. In real life, her personal experience with autism inspires other autistic people and helps foster greater understanding and acceptance of autism in general. The problem is that Grandin and others have made unproven and erroneous associations between autism and empathy for animals. There is actually little evidence that autistic people care about animals more or less than the rest of us. But even if there were, Grandin's statements to the press and in her own writing don't reveal a break from society's general acceptance of speciesism and animal exploitation. In the most predictable fashion, her love for her dogs translates into providing them with lifelong care and companionship while her alleged love for cows translates into accepting systematic violence as the norm. Rather than reveal anything unusual or unique about an autistic perspective on animal ethics, her position simply reflects the cultural norms that condition society to accept the vastly different standards we apply to such species as dogs and cows. Within the autistic community, in fact, there are diverse views on the issue, such as autistic and vegan Duncan Bachelor Dixon, who wrote on Facebook, "I don't think one has to love an animal, nor have compassion, in order to not kill them. . . . I am vegan because of recognizing injustice" (comment has since been deleted). Whether autism is a factor in shaping Grandin's views about farmed animals, popular culture nevertheless sees her as an animal advocate rather than the industry insider who designs livestock facilities, teaches animal science, and appears as a spokesperson for animal-industry trade organizations, otherwise known as the "humane" face of the industry.

Adding to this confusion, Temple Grandin's official website is a puzzle of conflicting ideas and positions on farmed animals that leaves us more perplexed about her conclusions than when we started. For instance, her position on what she calls "humane slaughter" and "appropriate" methods of slaughter begins not with an explanation of the benefits to the animal but of its economic/legal compliance advantages: "Stunning an animal correctly will provide better meat quality. Improper electric stunning will cause bloodspots in the meat and bone fractures. Good stunning practices are also required so that a plant will be in compliance with the Humane Slaughter Act. . . ."[100] But the HSA is essentially meaningless for at least 95 percent if not more of farmed animals since chickens, turkeys, ducks, and rabbits are intentionally exempted from the act. So she is only referring to cows here.

Compared to conventional methods of cow slaughter, Grandin claims her methods significantly reduce animal suffering. Still, Grandin's position underlies the assumption that killing animals for food is too sacred a practice to even call into question. Her reductionist logic ignores the insults and injuries endured by animals through breeding and raising them and focuses instead on making the last few minutes of their lives less terrifying. This assumption falls short of any serious, comprehensive consideration of all of the factors that impact the well-being and interests of farmed animals over the course of their natural lifespan.

One can't help but see the big elephant in the closet: If Grandin is truly the animal lover she claims to be, then why does she not advocate that animals be spared a life of exploitation and violence? Why not join the sanctuary movement to show the public how these same animals can be saved, protected, and appreciated for their intrinsic value, rather than valued only as commodities? Why instead does she choose to devote her life's work to more efficient forms of mass extermination? A 2013 New York Times Magazine interview reveals some answers to these questions. When asked if it troubles her to eat a steak, knowing what she knows about how animals are slaughtered, she replies, "No. I also think about the hyenas ripping the guts out of something, and that did not happen to that steak. The way the wolves kill things is not that nice. Cats will kill you first, but wolves just rip you open and dine on live guts."[101] So, according to this logic, we're morally superior for institutionalizing the exploitation and killing of animals we have no biological need to eat over those obligate carnivores who kill only to survive. Grandin's glib and illogical defense of eating animals is the same as those who have given little or no serious moral consideration of farmed animals, yet she frequently professes to being a genuine animal lover throughout her website. In some of her articles, she even seems to suggest that there is a moral basis for condemning animal exploitation altogether, based on her findings about animal behavior and intelligence. But then in other sections of the site, such as that pertaining to humane slaughter, she describes in chilling detail her "stairway to heaven" stunning and slaughter assembly-line, which she claims to be humane when compared to conventional practices that she views as decisively inhumane. In describing "proper" slaughter methods, she writes:

> In both captive bolt and electrically stunned animals, kicking will occur. Ignore the kicking and look at the head. To put it simply, THE HEAD MUST BE DEAD. When cattle are shot with a captive bolt, it is normal to have a spasm for 5 to 15 seconds. After the animal is rolled out of the box or hung up its eyes should relax and be wide open. After electrical stunning, a properly stunned animal should have a rigid (tonic) phase followed by a clonic (paddling of the legs) phase. This is an indication of a grand mal epileptic seizure. The seizure induces insensibility.[102]

For the animal victim, it's hard to imagine what such gradations of pain and suffering could mean, if anything, in the process of having his life snuffed out of him.

Some might argue that perhaps Grandin's popularity has awakened greater interest and concern for farmed animals, so that it is wrong to criticize her efforts to allegedly reduce animal suffering. Of course, most of us agree that less suffering is better than more suffering, but the question is whether Grandin's impact really reduces animal suffering, whether she has any impact at all on changing the cultural norms and beliefs that perpetuate animal exploitation, and perhaps most importantly, whether her impact ends up actually helping animal agriculture more than the animal victims of that system. Whatever the case, her popularity has resulted in at least three key advantages for animal agriculture: (1) More concerned consumers feeling better about eating what they perceive as more humanely raised flesh, dairy, and eggs, with even some vegetarians admitting to cheating, motivated by fictional humane slaughter marketing; (2) a humane face for an industry that is inherently and systematically violent; and (3) more efficient extermination technologies that improve that industry's bottom line, which even Grandin herself readily admits.

As evidence of her role as industry insider, we can find Grandin as a spokesperson for the American Meat Institute, the industry's leading lobby and public relations front group—narrating AMI's educational and promotional videos[103] and being featured prominently in their promotional literature such as *The Glass Walls Project*,[104] the industry's embarrassing attempt at a parody of the Sir Paul McCartney–narrated documentary *If Slaughterhouses Had Glass Walls*. In addition, Grandin has been a keynote speaker at the annual Animal Care and Handling Conference for the Food Industry. With Grandin at the helm, AMI has developed an "audit system and animal welfare guide" that has become the "global standard for animal welfare in the meat industry."[105] Grandin also appears in videos produced by the National Turkey Federation (the leading trade association for the turkey flesh industry), endorsing as humane certain handling procedures and gas extermination of turkeys. In stark contrast, other expert accounts of gassing birds claim that it is cheap and readily available and "causes the birds to burn, freeze, and suffocate to death simultaneously – and slowly."[108]

FARM OR FACTORY?

Grandin and others in the humane movement often frame the issue of farmed-animal welfare nostalgically as one in which we could return to simpler times when animals were treated better by family farmers instead of big corporate entities. But if we look at this issue more closely, we discover that a factory model of animal production is as old as civilization itself. An operation that can artificially incubate and hatch forty thousand chicken eggs into chicks per day most certainly qualifies as a "factory farm," yet we must travel over three thousand years back in time to ancient Egypt where some of the first high-production artificial incubators were developed. So, use of the term *factory farming*—which refers to the mass commodification of animals in an assembly-line environment (and all the horrors that go along with it)—falsely suggests that some viable alternative exists. The truth is that all commercial farming qualifies as factory farming based on an ancient production model of using animals as resource objects, with total control over their reproduction, the stealing and trafficking of their offspring, standard bodily mutilations (both physically and psychologically traumatizing), destruction of their families and social order, intensive biological manipulation and selective breeding, and of course the systematic domination, violence, and slaughter in their infancy or adolescence. All the above are necessary in any kind of farming to render their flesh and secretions into products of consumption.

Humane Claims That Mislead Consumers

"But I only buy humane animal products" is a response that has become more and more common as more people become aware of so-called "humane" labeled products and are led to believe they provide a solution for the conscious consumer. So let's go beyond the label to identify several important ways these humane claims are based on faulty logic and fictions.

The Unavoidable Paradox

The very existence of words like *free-range*, *cage-free* and *humane-certified* attests to the growing concern for farmed-animal welfare. But any time consumers of meat, eggs, or dairy advocate for "humane" treatment, they confront an unavoidable paradox: the movement to treat farm animals better is based on the idea that it is wrong to subject them to unnecessary harm, yet using and killing animals for their flesh and secretions when we have no need to eat them constitutes the ultimate act of unnecessary harm. When we have plentiful access to plant-based foods—and a choice between sparing life or taking it—there is nothing remotely humane about rejecting compassion and choosing violence and death for others just because we like the taste of their flesh, and because they cannot fight back. Might does not equal right.[109]

The Humane Double Standard

The dictionary definition of the word *humane* is having or showing compassion or benevolence. We apply this standard definition to our own species and to our companion animals, like cats and dogs, yet apply a vastly different standard to farmed animals. In fact, the routine practices of even the most "humane" farms would constitute torture and even atrocity if performed on human beings or companion animals. What logical explanation could there be to exempt just a handful of species—namely chickens, turkeys, cows, and pigs—from our customary humane standard? The fact is these animals possess the same fundamental capacity for suffering as our cats, our dogs, and ourselves.

False Humane Claims and False Dilemmas

Humane farming advocates claim to offer a clear alternative to "factory farming." There are at least three problems with this position. First, the differences aren't that significant. Many of the worst cruelties inflicted on animals in large industrial farms are also routine practices on small free-range farms. These include sexual violation and the exploitation of reproductive systems; the destruction of motherhood and families; routine mutilations without anesthetic; denial of the most fundamental behaviors and preferences; and brutal transport and slaughter conditions. Second, humane farming advocates frequently present a false dilemma, an either-or scenario, that misrepresents or outright ignores other important solutions to alleviate animal suffering. You can buy from us or factory farms, they claim. But in this context, eating animals is a given, a foregone conclusion. The third and most obvious choice—replacing animal products with satisfying plant-based alternatives—is intentionally ignored, yet would virtually eliminate unnecessary animal suffering altogether! Third, they compare their standards of animal handling with the worst, most abusive practices on large industrial farms, but anything looks better in such a comparison. In this case, better does not mean humane. Far from it. This mentality of trying to improve upon a practice that is inherently immoral is strikingly similar to the "mercy killing" and "euthanasia" programs of Nazi Germany, whereby gas extermination of millions of healthy adults and children was promoted as a "humane" alternative to shooting them point blank in the head and dumping their corpses into mass graves. To imply that mass extermination or genocide can be made humane is as ludicrous in the case of human atrocities as it is in the case of killing other animals because, let me repeat, we share the same fundamental capacity for suffering. Of course important differences between humans and other animals exist, but those differences don't justify exploiting, killing, and eating them.

The Ultimate Betrayal

Imagine for a moment how we would judge someone who devised a plan to win the trust of a child only to betray that child by violently taking his life. And imagine that the perpetrator's intent was to make a profit off of that victim's body. Would we look for reasons to come to the perpetrator's defense, saying perhaps that at least the child lived a good life? Or would we say that at least the child didn't know what was going to happen to him? Of course not. A perpetrator who premeditates a murder so as to benefit from that person's death is considered far more culpable in the eyes of the law, and thus his punishment is more severe. The same is true when animals are visibly victimized. When we hear about, for instance, someone who tortured and killed a cat for kicks and then posted a video on YouTube, or a boyfriend who retaliated against his ex-girlfriend by killing her dog, or the discovery of a cockfighting ring, we are outraged and demand justice. This reaction is based on our belief that harming others without just cause is categorically wrong. And harming animals, particularly in the name of pleasure, offends our sensibilities.

Now consider the case of the "humane" farmer who claims to foster a caring and trusting relationship with his animals, treating them with kindness and respect, sometimes even naming them. His animals may respond in kind, bonding with and perhaps even becoming affectionate with their caretaker. But all along, the farmer has ulterior motives to kill them so he can butcher and sell their dismembered parts as soon as they develop to a certain size and weight. All along, his intention is to artificially breed them into this world only to slaughter them in their infancy or adolescence to profit from products procured from their flesh or bodily secretions that are unnecessary for human health. In no way does this constitute a humane intention, let alone a humane act. Again, in the words of author Hope Bohanec, "the more humanely an animal is treated, the greater is the bond of trust, and the greater the bond of trust, the more severe the crime of betrayal."[106] What Bohanec refers to is the ultimate betrayal, a betrayal not just to the animal but also to our most deeply held values of justice, reciprocity, and respect for others.

Beyond Humane Treatment

As emphasized earlier, "humane" farming tries to keep the focus of attention squarely on humane treatment, but how an animal is treated during the short time he is permitted to stay alive is only part of the equation for evaluating the overall quality of an animal's life. There are other, unavoidable forms of suffering that are inflicted on farmed animals beyond the issue of treatment. With every animal product we buy, we contribute to the following inhumane circumstances.

The Inhumanity of Breeding

We have intensively bred and biologically manipulated today's breeds of farmed animals to "optimize" their milk and egg production and flesh tissue growth, exacting a heavy toll on their bodies and resulting in abnormalities, diseases, and premature death. As a result, many are frail and highly susceptible to disease. Weak, sickly, or injured animals are a liability to farmers who will not incur the high cost of treating the medical condition of an individual animal; instead, they will be taken out of production and either left to die or sent to slaughter. Again, consider the vastly different ethical standard we apply to our own species: we oppose, both on principle and in practice, experimentation on or biological manipulation of the human body that knowingly causes harm, particularly when it is conducted covertly and without our consent.

The Inhumanity of Commodification

Use is indeed abuse. Being used as a resource against their will for someone else's gain causes great physical and psychological suffering to animals who demonstrate their desire to live freely and who resist being dominated and denied the ability to express their essential interests and preferences. Any type of farming guarantees that animals are to be stripped of their freedom and subjugated to the will of their owners. The inhumanity of commodification is further reinforced culturally and linguistically when we refer to an animal as "meat" or some other consumer product. Words like *meat* intentionally strip animals of their identity, dignity, and value beyond the commodification of their flesh.

The Inhumanity of Taking a Life

The gravest harm to any animal is not treating him badly, but taking his life. In agriculture, animals' lives are taken violently and cut drastically short. Animals can recover from some harms, but death is permanent. To follow the argument of humane-farming advocates to its logical conclusion, if how we treat animals matters, then their very lives matter even more, not less. Nothing matters more to a sentient being with a subjective sense of self-awareness than his own life, which he will fiercely fight to protect.

THE BACKYARD HEN FANTASY

Okay, well, maybe all commercial farming is inherently exploitative and violent, but surely backyard chicken keeping is an ethical way to have eggs, isn't it? Laying eggs is clearly what defines these birds for most people. Even otherwise well-informed people are under the spell of contrived and false egg-industry perceptions of chickens. Sanctuaries often get asked, "What is the harm of eating the eggs of backyard chickens who will just lay them anyway?" In fact, many chicken keepers claim that they have a symbiotic relationship with their hens. In exchange for good treatment, they see their "reward" as the eggs that their chickens lay. Sounds like a win-win situation, but we will see later in detail why this logic does not pan out. In order to fully understand our impact on these birds, we must look way beyond treatment.

The Harm of the Hatcheries

Let's start where nearly all chicks are born: in hatcheries. When we buy chicks, we are directly and financially supporting hatcheries that are responsible for a whole host of staggeringly cruel practices. Their most egregious offense is the maceration (grinding up alive) and suffocation of billions of baby male chicks—six billion globally every year. Those who adopt or rescue backyard chickens instead of buying from hatcheries withdraw their support from the hatcheries but still face several important ethical considerations in answering the question "What's the harm in collecting and eating the eggs that our adopted chickens lay?"

The Harm of Breeding

Chickens bred for egg laying are irreparably harmed by the selective breeding that has forced them to lay an unnatural and unhealthy number of eggs (between 250 to 300 a year), resulting in a host of painful and life-threatening reproductive diseases and premature death. Consider the fact that most egg-laying hens, even the so-called heritage breeds, will only live four to six years on average (assuming they are allowed to live past their one- to two-year egg-laying prime) and will likely die of complications caused by egg laying. In contrast, undomesticated chicken hens living in their natural habitat have been known to live thirty years and more. They lay eggs just like other wild birds do (for purposes of reproduction) and only a few clutches per year—around ten to fifteen eggs total on average.

Benefiting from Harm

There is a well-established legal concept called Fruit of the Poisonous Tree, which can be applied to the consumption of chicken eggs as well as the secretions and flesh of other animals. As Sherry Colb explains, "If someone has committed a wrong in acquiring some product, . . . it is wrongful to utilize and enjoy the 'benefits' of that product just as it was wrongful to commit the harm that resulted in the product's acquisition in the first place. In other words, one becomes an accomplice in the initial wrongdoing by taking the fruits of that wrongdoing and utilizing them as a source of pleasure, information, etc."[107] In fact, our justice system recognizes that gaining some pleasure or benefit from the source of someone else's suffering is immoral. We would consider it objectionable to, say, rescue a dog used in a dogfighting ring and argue that, since he is already trained and bred to fight, in exchange for adopting him and providing him refuge, we allow him to fight other dogs and place bets on him. Or perhaps we let him be a guard dog somewhere that could potentially put him in harm's way. He might as well "earn his keep" since he's going to be a fighter anyway. But of course we would never use this logic with a rescued dog. Even if we are not the direct cause of the chicken's suffering, by eating her eggs, we are benefiting from what harms her; that is, her "rigged" reproduction, which would not even be possible without the industrial scale genetic manipulation and breeding practices we already claim to oppose, on the grounds that they are horrifically cruel.

Exploitation Logic Applied to Backyard Chickens

Backyard chicken keepers often portray their relationship with their chickens as a win-win situation. They provide their chickens with a great life, and in return their chickens provide them with eggs. There are at least two problems with this position. First, it ignores the fact these eggs exist only because of the systematic manipulation and re-engineering of the chicken hen's reproductive system, which forces her to produce an unnatural and unhealthy amount of eggs. Second, it is impossible for chickens to give their consent to such an arrangement. It assumes that they desire to make a sacrifice for us, but in reality, their intensive egg laying—and the adverse consequences that come with it—is forced upon them by no choice of their own. But what if we adopt or rescue backyard chickens? Well, as author Charles Horn points out, "If the desire is there to eat the eggs, did that consciously or subconsciously go into the decision to adopt in the first place? If so, the intention was never just one of providing refuge; it was also one of exploitation."[110] This whole exercise of seeking out rare situations in which it might be considered ethical to eat the eggs of adopted chickens opens the door to other exceptions being made. "If it's okay to eat," Horn posits, "is it okay to gather and sell? Is it okay to adopt many chickens and make a business out of it? Again, we're seeing how we still have a mindset of exploitation here and just how easily the slippery slope can lead people toward animal agriculture. If not them, someone else surely will, because the mindset of exploitation is still there."[111]

Identifying as an "Egg Eater"

Identifying ourselves as "egg eaters" creates a domino effect, which is fueled by at least four realities that work together to cause the domino effect:

1. We send a powerful message of affirmation to others simply by eating eggs, regardless of their source—even those laid by the hens in our backyard.

2. Egg-industry marketing has tried and tested methods of seducing well-intentioned and caring consumers and fabricating feel-good brands and stories that will falsely suggest that their eggs come from places like our backyard.

3. Most consumers are still grossly misinformed about egg farming and cruelty to animals, and egg marketers use this to their advantage.

4. Consumers have a powerful incentive to believe in the humane myth with which these marketers manipulate us, with their feel-good packaging, signs, and advertising at the point of purchase that resemble or allude to the kind of conditions that we associate with backyard settings.

The sad reality is that most caring consumers targeted by this marketing buy into the myth, both literally and figuratively. Or they order eggs in a breakfast eatery where happy hen motifs adorn the walls, and they falsely associate this experience with a backyard hen scene, when, in reality, even the most upscale restaurants get eggs from hens raised in deplorable cage conditions. As Hope Bohanec points out, "When someone eats eggs from their own hens, they then identify as an egg-eater and don't limit their consumption of eggs to just the supposed 'ethical' eggs from their hens. They will eat other eggs as well in a restaurant, at a friend's house, etc., so they are still supporting the cruel egg industry, even though they may identify as only eating 'ethical' eggs, it is unlikely that those are the only eggs they are eating."[112]

Reinforcing the False Egg-Industry Stereotype

Eating the eggs of backyard chickens also reinforces their egg-industry role as "layers" or egg-laying machines, as if to suggest that this is their primary purpose in life, which is incorrect. The fact is that natural egg laying for chickens is no different than it is for many other birds. What's changed is that modern breeding has forced chickens to produce an obscene amount of infertile eggs. As discussed in chapter 2, beyond egg laying, chickens lead rich and complex social lives, have many interests, and are keenly self-aware. They have long-term memory and clearly demonstrate that they anticipate future events. They form deep bonds with other flock mates and other species, like dogs and humans. And yet even if they didn't possess all of these advanced cognitive abilities, they are sentient beings who feel pain and pleasure much like we do. And sentience, not intelligence, is the basis for how we should treat others. By eating eggs, we imply that the worth of chickens amounts to what they can produce for us as a food source, rather than focusing attention where it should be: on chickens' intrinsic worth as individuals. "Just as we don't see human beings or human secretions as a food source, similarly we shouldn't see any sentient being or their secretions that way either," writes Charles Horn.[113]

What to Do with the Eggs?

While wasting is covered in its own section, it's inevitable in any discussion of backyard hens that someone will argue it is wrong to waste chickens' eggs by not eating them. When we let go of the anthropocentric notion that chickens' eggs belong to us, then what could we potentially do with the eggs, if we instead wanted to do something to benefit these most exploited of birds? Well, we can hard-boil the eggs and grind up the shells. We can add the shells to the chickens' grit to give them back some of the vast amounts of calcium that is leached from their bones to produce all of those shells. We can also feed their eggs back to them in order to restore some of the protein and other nutrients they lose in the process of laying far more eggs than their bodies were ever intended to produce. Putting harm aside, we might want to stop and think about what kind of relationships we are cultivating with our backyard chickens as well as what message we are sending out to the world. Must every relationship we have be contingent upon getting something in return? Sometimes we can just show kindness and compassion. Sometimes we can just appreciate others for their intrinsic worth and not base their value on what we can get out of them. And in the case of chickens, this could never be more desperately needed, considering all of the suffering we force upon some forty billion of them around the world every year for our taste buds.

Chapter 5:

Fictionalizing Animal Identities

An important strategy in the propaganda used to oppress inferior groups is a concerted assault on the identity of those groups. The fictions of animal identity covered in this chapter have been enormously successful at distancing us from the animals we exploit. If we think of farmed animals at all, we are most likely rationalizing away why they don't matter, why they shouldn't be given the same consideration as other animals, and even why they deserve their fate.

INVISIBILITY

Social psychologist Melanie Joy identifies *invisibility* as an important mechanism for maintaining the dominant carnistic culture. It is no accident that we rarely, if ever, meet those who are being misrepresented: the animals. They are conveniently hidden from public view. Consider the fact that at any given time, there are approximately thirty-two farmed animals being raised for every American. Think about how many people you see on a daily basis—in person, on television, on the Internet, etc. In Joy's analysis, "the main defense mechanism of carnism is denial which is expressed largely through invisibility. For instance, 1.2 billion farmed animals are slaughtered globally every week. But how many of these animals have you seen? Where are they?"[114] Author Carol Adams refers to this invisibility of the animal victim as the absent referent: "Behind every meal of meat is an absence: the death of the animal whose place the meat takes. . . . The absent referent functions to cloak the violence inherent to meat eating, to protect the conscience of the meat eater and render the idea of individual animals as immaterial to anyone's selfish desires. It is that which separates the meat eater from the animal and the animal from the end product . . . to allow for the moral abandonment of another being."[115]

If animals remain invisible to us or mere abstractions represented by images of massive populations of "Frankenclones," our relationship to them remains severed and our apathy intact. We don't see the terror on their faces. We don't hear their cries of distress and desperation. We don't read their body language of physical and emotional resistance to domination. We never experience their struggle against pain, suffering, and death. If this reality was properly framed in our minds each time it was imposed upon them and for each meal of ours that required it, the dysfunction of our denial response would be overwhelming and perhaps even overcome, resulting in far less animal consumption. The powerful process of moving from the invisible to the visible seems to hold true for disenfranchised or oppressed human groups as well, where empathy seems to improve when we identify more intimately with an individual from such a group.[116]

Of course, particularly in the early phases of a social movement, society generally reacts to calls to end an injustice by either denying or justifying its existence. And even those movements that have enjoyed widespread and mainstream acceptance still meet resistance. There are still Holocaust deniers, homophobes, and climate deniers. Often there is a conspiracy of invisibility and silence that cloaks an injustice, until those seeking to remedy it can no longer be kept silent or invisible. At that point, the question becomes not whether people will listen or care, but whether the growing chorus of dissent imposes societal pressures necessary to make a change. At the same time, the truth about farmed animals is more visible and accessible than ever before. Anyone can quickly and easily access undercover footage inside animal farms and slaughterhouses on the Internet. The fact that so many still insulate themselves in an "I don't want to know" state of self-deception seems to suggest that the fictional power of invisibility is to some extent bidirectional. As stated earlier in the book, we tell the food industry what we believe and want to see and hear, and the industry projects that back to us through clever branding executions. In a recent study of consumer perceptions of certain animal-product brands, Scandinavian researchers describe consumers as "active partners in creating the illusion of animal welfare."[117] In describing the fictional dynamic between the producer and the consumer, they show how "'willed blindness' allows them [consumers] to close their eyes to the reality of animal production . . . reinforced by the commercials."[118] In emphasizing the bidirectional nature of fiction-telling, these researchers conclude that "the co-operation between producers and consumers to maintain the idea of Old McDonald's farm, despite clear evidence to the contrary, is . . . one of the most important challenges of animal welfare."[119]

ANONYMITY

When we do see farmed animals, they are often portrayed as nameless, faceless, generic, and lacking any unique or differentiating qualities. Anonymity is another fictional device that strips animals of their own unique identity or personality. The posters we see hanging up on the wall at the butcher shop or meat section of the grocery store is a common example. Here a silhouetted profile of an animal is presented with lines going through the different parts of his body to represent the different cuts of meat. Similarly, generic illustrations of hens often appear on egg cartons and egg products, pigs on pork products, and cows on dairy products. Anonymous portraits of animals prevent us from making any real or meaningful connection with them. Some research also shows the opposite to also be true: the more we become enchanted by the unique qualities in someone, human or nonhuman animal, the deeper is our reverence, interest, and respect for them, as well as our desire to help them.[120] A more subtle but no less powerful form of anonymity is found in the media's portrayal of animals as mass populations via images of large herds and flocks in which it would be impossible to ascertain the individual nature of any one animal photographed.

TRIVIALIZATION

When animals are not invisible or portrayed as anonymous, popular culture often trivializes them and their incredible misfortune of being born into a human-dominated world that regards them as mere resources, by misrepresenting them as clownish cartoon characters or macabre caricatures. Trivialization often uses mockery to further sabotage any serious consideration for animals and the suffering we cause them. If we can laugh at them, then we don't have to take the suffering we cause them seriously. Prime examples of this are The Laughing Cow cheese brand and the countless BBQ restaurant graphics composed of funny-looking pigs. We also use trivialization as a coping or defense mechanism, a kind of knee-jerk "Mmm, bacon" reaction. We trivialize the stark life and death circumstances we impose on other animals by claiming that it would be worse to insult a human cook than inflict suffering and death on the animal (to protect the cook's ego, of course). For example, in an interview with *Playboy*, celebrity chef Anthony Bourdain complains about how "they [vegetarians] make for bad travelers and bad guests. The notion that before you even set out to go to Thailand, you say, 'I'm not interested,' or you're unwilling to try things that people take so personally and are so proud of and so generous with, I don't understand that, and I think it's rude. You're at Grandma's house, you eat what Grandma serves you."[121] One wonders how far Bourdain would take that logic. Would he eat human flesh if it was served to him by a grandma from a cannibalistic tribe? Would he accept cultures in which Grandma performs genital mutilation or human sacrifice? Or do we just accept Grandma's kind and well-intentioned gestures in cases of satisfying our palate pleasures, when the suffering of those who have no say can be easily ignored?

A similar line of reasoning based on selective moral relativism is used in certain strains of Buddhism where guidelines for food choices are dictated by eating what the host serves you so as not to insult the host. If the host serves you animal flesh, even though Buddhism generally compels you to vegetarianism, it is considered socially acceptable to eat the animal's flesh out of respect for the host or to avoid wasting the animal's body. According to the Tibetan Buddhist Monastery and Centre for World Peace and Health, there are three specific circumstances under which eating the flesh of animals can be considered "clean" and therefore acceptable: "First, I did not see with my own eyes that the animal was killed for me; second, I did not hear from someone I trust that it was killed specifically for me; third, I myself have no doubt that it was not killed specially for me. For example, the meat sold at the market is for all meat eaters, not for me alone, so it is to be deemed clean meat or, when being the guest of a Tibetan house, the hosts would usually kill a sheep to honour their guest."[122] If we apply this to our own circumstances, we can see how these allegedly exceptional cases actually cover the vast majority of the meals we eat, including all meals made from purchased meat and meat served to us in a restaurant or any function we attend. The only time it would be considered unethical, by these standards, would be when we go out and kill our own animals for food. The net effect of these and other exceptions to vegetarianism is to trivialize the plight of animals by further reinforcing their status as objects of consumption.

DENIGRATION

We've developed a whole vocabulary of animal words used to disparage, insult, or denigrate others. We call each other "fat cows," "worms" (who have no courage), and "pigs" (who have no manners). One of the *Merriam-Webster* dictionary definitions of the word *chicken* is "a person who is afraid."[123] In the iconic new-wave film *Rebel Without a Cause*, the plot centers around the power of peer pressure, bullying, and the stigma of the chicken/coward complex. In the pinnacle scene in the film, the protagonist Jim Stark (played by James Dean) is challenged to a game called the "chicken run," a dangerous stunt that involves driving cars off the side of a cliff. The first one who jumps out of the car loses and is designated the "chicken." Stark begrudgingly accepts the challenge after taunting from his classmates who call him a chicken. In the next scene, he confesses the incident to his mother and father, who are mortified by what he has done. Again he admits to them that he couldn't bear the chicken/coward stigma from his peers.

Contrary to popular culture's relentless attack on the chicken's character, chickens are widely known to exhibit incredible bravery and altruism. Roosters display valiant courage in protecting their flock. Mother hens fiercely protect their young, often willing to risk their own lives in the process. Alpha females and males are known to be protective of the more submissive members of their flock, acting as decoys and putting themselves in great danger with predators for the benefit of the flock. The head rooster protects the territory the group inhabits, as well as the chicks and hens in the group. Groups are composed of more dominant hens who remain close to the head rooster as well as more submissive hens and roosters who keep to the periphery.[124] But in *Rebel Without a Cause*, the chicken is the loser, the coward, the persecuted one, the weaker one, the inferior one. The chicken's identity is turned upside down. And denigrating chickens makes it easier to justify exploiting and killing them as a resource.

VICTIM BLAMING

How popular culture portrays animal victims is enormously important to understanding why we victimize them in the first place. Recent research in social psychology explores how believing that life is fair can make us apathetic to victims.[125] Beginning in the 1960s, research has shown that if we feel powerless to alleviate an injustice, we have a tendency to convince ourselves that the victims deserve their fate. This has important implications for understanding our collective denial and indifference to the massive scale of farmed-animal suffering. Victim blaming can appear as innocuous as the friendly family dairy farmer of Orange Patch Dairy in Minnesota, who wrote a lengthy response to a vegan who had concerns about taking mother cows away from their calves. In his blog post, he explains that once a calf is delivered, the mother may walk away without licking the calf clean, instead moving directly to the feed bunk. The calf would then be left to die, cold and wet. But if the farmer was really intent on helping the baby imprint on his mother and be accepted by his mother, there are many things he could try. Instead, the farmer's intention is not to help them bond. On the contrary, he needs to break that maternal bond because he makes a living on that mother's milk, the milk that was intended by nature for her calf. One million male calves are disposed of by dairy farmers every year in the United States because they have no value to dairy farmers. It's in bad faith that they blame the mothers for being "bad mothers" and use the fact that some mothers might abandon their calves as a justification to systematically break up their families so that they can traffic their offspring and exploit them for their milk.

Large or small, farmers often blame the animal victim, citing the animal's bad behavior as a reason to exploit them for profit. Emily Meredith, communications director for the Animal Agriculture Alliance, has a column on the Meatingplace.com website called *Activist Watch*. In a series of articles called "My Week on a 'Fact'ory Farm: Part I," Meredith chronicles her trip to a large sow breeding facility somewhere in the Midwest and writes, "No matter the industry practices I observed that first day—from tail docking to castration to artificial insemination—that theme of respect carried through. I saw no 'factory' and all farm — just workers who took great pride in being the best herdsmen to happy, healthy and well cared for animals."[126] Later in the article Meredith defends gestation crates, pointing out how hostile and stressed the sows become when they are not in their gestation crates and instead allowed to interact with each other in intensely confined environments. Like the small dairy farmer, she blames the victim and ignores the real possibility that such aggressive behavior might have something to do with the unnatural conditions to which we subject these animals. One can only imagine if these were human mothers instead of sows living in these conditions.

Animal victim blaming is commonly found in the media where animals are routinely blamed for problems entirely created by us, like the spread of bird flu and PED piglet virus. In numerous articles about PEDV published by Reuters, experts were interviewed and quoted, including Steve Meyer, president of the consulting firm Paragon Economics, who told Reuters that "the virus could tighten U.S. pork supplies in about five to six months by causing the deaths of baby pigs."[127] The language is key in supporting the denial of responsibility for the source of the problem: the breeding and raising of pigs for profit by hog farmers. You don't blame those hard-working farmers for anything. It's not politically correct to blame people who feed us bacon and ribs and ham we so love. In the media's coverage of the virus, what's missing is the fact that PEDV is a disease that was allowed to thrive and rapidly spread due to the way we breed and confine pigs today in modern agriculture. The victims are not the pig farmers and their economic losses, as the coverage asserts. The victims are the animals themselves. The pig farmers are the perpetrators of the animals' suffering. They create victims as a business model. And all of this not because there is a gun to our head to eat bacon but just because we like the taste so much we're willing to go to absurd extremes to protect the economic interests of those who profit from this mess. The PEDV epidemic is a case in point for how we create our own problems with animals. We breed them into a world of human tyranny, blame them for "spreading diseases," and then destroy their offspring to stop the spread of disease.

And then there is the variation on victim blaming we see from the so-called progressive food movement leaders. In a 2012 interview in *Smithsonian*, Michael Pollan described his experience with raising chickens: "Their brains have been bred right out of them, they're really nasty and stupid."[128] But ask anyone who has rescued these baby birds and they'll describe how sweet and gentle they are. Pollan's disdain for chickens is the same one held by the very industrial food industry that Pollan claims to adamantly oppose. With sustainable, "food revolution" types like Pollan talking trash about animals and devaluing them in exactly the same way as agribusiness, is it any wonder that chickens are treated as trash? By blaming the victims, Pollan predictably falls prey to the conventional meathead logic: the animal is so nasty and stupid, he doesn't deserve to live.

If Pollan were serious about his opposition to industrial agriculture, he would not be raising chickens who were selectively bred by industrial hatcheries to grow freakishly fast into adult bodies in forty-two days. Whether he realizes it or not, he learned his disdain for the victims from the poultry industry itself. The rejection of "Frankenbirds" would be logically consistent with his critique of industrial agriculture. Instead, Pollan trashes the chickens. Even if chickens were truly "stupid and nasty," what does this have to do with how we treat others? Do we only treat those who are "smart and sweet" with a modicum of respect and instead cut off the heads of those we deem less intelligent or lovable? Don't we ourselves become "stupid and nasty" when we decide, arbitrarily, that someone else deserves to be abused and exploited because we don't like them? We denigrate animals who can't defend themselves as "stupid and nasty" when we want to do something bad to them; in this case, when someone like Michael Pollan wants to cut off their heads or stuff them through a kill cone and slit their throats, just to say he's done it. Then he can tell the press how clueless vegans are about where their food comes from.

Victim Identification

We often see stories of human or nonhuman animal victims in which a campaign to help just one individual was hugely successful. Hunger relief organizations often successfully appeal to donors by telling compelling stories of individual children in need that you can sponsor. Identifying with an individual victim, whether human or nonhuman, becomes fictional when we can't relate how their individual experience connects with a larger problem that, in reality, encompasses massive populations of human and other animal victims. Take, for example, the September 2014 news story of a dog in Kentucky named Felicity, who was found tied to a post and branded with a profanity. Her story sparked an outpouring of empathy as well as outrage and indignation for the perpetrators. The local humane society in Lexington raised money from many donors in honor of her rescue, and a vet even volunteered to perform plastic surgery to cover up the profanity branded into her skin. The Lexington Humane Society also issued a $3,500 reward for those who led them to Felicity's abuser. Many are baffled at why someone would want to do this to an innocent animal. And yet, as horrible as this is, it is not without precedent. In fact, branding has been used routinely for centuries to identify both nonhuman animals and even human slaves.

While the story of Felicity's branding with a profanity is sad and shocking, it shines a light on the fact that branding, and numerous other cruel and inhumane mutilations, are routinely practiced on billions of farmed animals every year, on small and large farms alike. Not only are farmed animals branded, they are subjected to other painful bodily mutilations as infants without anesthesia, including castration, dehorning, tail docking (cutting off their tails), debeaking, the cutting down and extraction of teeth, the cutting off of toes, and ear notching (cutting out pieces of a pig's ears). The branding of farmed animals can be traced back to ancient Egypt. Mexican cattle ranchers were known to mark their cattle with their family coat of arms. The reason for branding animals throughout history was to make it clear who the animal belonged to.

The branding of human slaves also has a long history that some historians believe is connected to the practice of enslaving other animals.[129] Ancient Romans marked runaway slaves with the letters *FUG* (for "fugitives"). European and American colonial slave traders branded millions of slaves during the period of transatlantic enslavement. Southern slave owners often branded slaves' palms, shoulders, buttocks, or cheeks with a branding iron, giving them permanent identifying marks should they escape and be caught. Some prisoners of Auschwitz were tattooed with numbers on their arms. In contemporary times, certain gangs and other groups brand their members as a rite of initiation into the group. International animal liberation movement 269Life, in fact, makes the act of branding a central symbol of its fight to end animal oppression. In the words of founder Sasha Boojor, "it's a method that humanity invented to take away an individual's personality and identity. We believe that animal activists who willingly subject themselves to branding undermine its mainstream legitimacy."[130] Aside from burning a mark or number into the skin, there are others forms of identification used on farmed animals today that are equally disturbing. A recent undercover investigation at an Australian farm exposed female breeding sows ("baby machines") with the words "destroy" and "lame, cull" spray painted across the sides of their bodies.

REVERSE VICTIMIZATION

When not blaming animal victims, popular culture is busy crafting elaborate fictions portraying ourselves as the victims of the problems we created. In the Western states, ranchers and farmers identify themselves as victims of wildlife who threaten their farmed animals and therefore their bottom line. They lobby the government to protect their interests and promote hunting—yet another industry that profits on animal suffering and loss of lives, all at the expense of taxpayers.

Agribusiness also fashions itself as a victim—a victim of the animal protection movement. The 2013 annual stakeholder's meeting for the Animal Agriculture Alliance (AAA) in May is entitled "Activists at the Door: Protecting Animals, Farms, Food & Consumer Confidence." The expansive animal rights section of the AAA website features a subsection entitled "Agriculture is Outnumbered, Outfunded by Animal Activists." It's becoming increasingly evident that the perceived threat of activism to agribusiness and one of its key lobbying groups, AAA, factors heavily into their concerns.

The "animal rights" section of the AAA website displays animal activists as if they are public enemies. "Radical activist organizations are leading the fight to grant animals the same legal rights as humans,"[131] the site claims, but when was the last time you heard animal activists campaigning for an animal's right to vote, to gay marriage, to abortion, or to equal housing opportunities? Their intent is clearly to misrepresent the clear position that animals should have the fundamental right not be used as an agricultural resource. AAA uses political smear tactics akin to how a whistleblower group might campaign to expose corporate crime and corruption, framing the advocacy of animals as a criminal activity. To illustrate this, they've created an elaborate flowchart, what they call their "Activist Map," displaying all of the major animal activist groups and how they are connected through financial support, according to AAA. In addition, there are at least fourteen profile pages on what AAA sees as the top animal organizations. Following the offenders' profiles is a long string of news excerpts, many of which "expose" major corporations and brands that have shown their allegiance to some animal groups, as if to suggest they are engaging in illicit activity by supporting animal charities. One of these news items urges farmers to practice extreme caution when hiring staff. You just might unintentionally hire a radical who will take undercover video and expose your mistreatment of animals or even the everyday, "normal" standards of practice that are often no less disturbing. "The activist tactic of obtaining illicit employment at a farm or processing plant in order to acquire video intended to malign the reputation of farmers and ranchers is becoming increasingly common," the AAA website warns.[132] But this statement begs the question: If there is nothing bad going on, then what do these facilities have to lose or hide by having video recorded there? In addition, the AAA has a dossier on many individuals it is tracking and making their profiles and photos available on their site so that farmers can check against the applicants they are considering. It's like a caricature of *America's Most Wanted*. The paranoid worldview of organizations like AAA become the same as those reflected in everyday people, such as the Facebook user and former 4-H club member who commented on a post, "If we didn't eat farmed animals, they would eat us."

VICTIM DENIAL

As a general matter, our culture teaches us that only humans can be victims. We use victim denial as a fictional device, often without realizing it, when we express an attitude of human exceptionalism about what is "proper" treatment for other animals, or when we pretend that only humans are worthy of justice or freedom from harm, or when we claim that justice for us at the expense of other animals is inevitable, rather than a false competitive construct between ourselves and other species. Even if we believe that humans are "superior" to other animals—whatever the arbitrary, self-serving basis is for making the claim—it does not justify treating animals in any way we see fit any more than the discriminatory claim of white superiority translates into enslaving, exploiting, and lynching people of color. Unfortunately, the use of disconnection as a fictional device is so widespread, we can find examples of it even within the social justice community. For example, an organization that calls itself Chicken Justice actually does nothing to help alleviate the suffering of chickens.[133] Their website describes their work as "a project of Interfaith Worker Justice, which has been a leader in the fight for economic and worker justice in the U.S. since 1996. IWJ mobilizes people of faith and worker advocates in support of economic justice and worker rights at the local, state and national levels. . . . IWJ supports workers in poultry and meat processing factories, who are doing some of the most dangerous, low-paid work while providing the food for U.S. dinner tables."[134] It's hard to imagine how anyone concerned about injustice could be blind to the egregious suffering of the forty billion bird victims of the poultry industry and focus exclusively on those who work within the industry itself. Perhaps Chicken Justice might instead focus their efforts on helping slaughterhouse workers get out of those horrifying work environments and find work elsewhere, thereby helping workers and not further contributing to our betrayal of animal victims.

Some animal advocates believe that we shouldn't fight society's apathy over animal suffering and instead take an easier, more practical route. "People don't care about animals," they say. "It's better to emphasize the health and environmental benefits instead since that's what people care about." But ignoring the victim is the problem, not the solution. From a historical context, it is only when a small vocal minority begins breaking through the silence and denial about an injustice, not by continuing to ignore it, that change occurs. Ignoring or protecting or pandering to those in denial is not a strategy for change. Animal advocates are charged with the task of making the case for why people should care and using creative strategies for getting society's attention, and there are compelling arguments for why people should care about other animals. There is also ample evidence that most people do care yet haven't acted on it on the level we would hope. It's up to us to connect the dots between beliefs and actions.

AUTHENTICITY

The dairy, egg, and meat industries have been promoting their products as the real thing and plant alternatives as fakes for a very long time. This brainwashing has worked incredibly well on most of us, who buy into their fictional distortions of what foods we perceive as real or fake. The dairy industry's REAL Seal is a classic example of this authenticity fiction, a fiction which is often built upon a long history or tradition of a certain practice or phenomenon. In terms of food, eating plants has been around at least as long or longer than eating animals. So the idea that animal products are real while plant alternatives are fake has no basis in truth. The authenticity fictions become amplified in the dairy sector where viable plant-based alternatives for milk and other dairy products have emerged to pose a formidable threat to the dairy sector's market share. Ironically, the process of breeding, raising, and killing animals today is about as unreal and artificial as it gets. What is authentic about the experience of picking up food products off of the store shelf? When we consider how few people have any contact with the living animals who are violently rendered into food, it's laughable that these same consumers believe in authentic fictions from animal agriculture. They are about as far removed from the source of their food as humanly possible. Of course, this does not mean that the inverse situation is ethical. Knowing where and how your animal products come to the table does not in itself make the same violent process ethical. And that is the subject of the next fiction.

Visibility

In the so-called sustainable/humane food movement, the popular slogan "Know where your food comes from" often translates into witnessing or partaking in violence against animals as a path toward ethical eating. The fiction that portrays this act as somehow making us more courageous, conscious, aware, or even ethically superior than others is what I call visibility. In one sense, it is a reaction to exposing the widespread invisibility of farmed animals in our culture discussed earlier. Urban Adamah, a Jewish organization that runs an animal farm and offers kosher chicken slaughter classes, preserves violent and harmful traditions. But in preserving these rituals, they also promote the visibility fiction through statements such as this one from a kosher slaughterer, Yadidya Greenberg: "I have seen time and again that witnessing live slaughter is a great way to engage people and get them asking questions."[135] But do we ask the fundamental question of why we believe it's okay to do this to a chicken but not, say, to a cat? What if it were a cat, instead of a chicken, callously grasped by his legs, hung upside, and his throat slashed? Would we consider this an "engaging" conversation piece that raises important questions, or would we condemn this as the gratuitous killing of an innocent animal? Groups like Urban Adamah ignore the fundamental contradiction behind the social acceptability of doing this to chickens—who, incidentally, have no laws to protect them from cruelty or violence—but not to an animal like a cat, who has laws sufficient to prosecute the perpetrator for committing the same act. Speciesism is the prejudice that allows us to regard some species as valuable enough to protect and others as having no value, whose lives are disposable because we say so. Anyone on a path to greater consciousness should think critically and seriously about speciesism as a foundation for understanding animal ethics and prejudice as a general matter.

The shoddy logic revealed in the Urban Adamah slaughterer's statement insists that we must witness or even partake in rituals of violence and killing for people to understand why violence and killing is bad, as if we don't already know instinctually that suffering and death is bad, because sentient beings seek to avoid suffering and death at all costs. When it comes to evaluating atrocities and violations committed against human beings, we don't engage in debate over whether it is right or wrong. We accept on principle, and do not require further evidence, that it is wrong for the victims and therefore immoral. And when we do see further evidence of atrocities, we immediately comprehend the horror and suffering and appropriately conclude that such acts are categorically wrong. We wouldn't wish this on our own worst enemies. So why do we need a live demonstration of animals crying out and thrashing in agony as their necks are cut and bodies draining of blood to convince people of the reality of their suffering? And to carry this idea to its logical conclusion, how many animals would need to be sacrificed to educate a burgeoning human population into recognizing just how awful slaughter is?

Even if one believed that this kind of training could have a positive impact on people, exactly how could this model be scaled up to serve anything more than just an elite niche of consumers? As author Hope Bohanec explains,

> at any given time, there are 100 million head of
> cattle and 70 million pigs alive in the U.S. Current-

ly, only about 9 percent of all livestock is pasture raised. How would we ever have the land to pasture raise them all? To give all farmed animals the space they need to have even a semblance of a natural life, we would have to destroy millions more acres of wild areas, forests, prairies, and wetlands to accommodate them. There is not enough land on the planet, or even two planets, to free-range all the billions of pigs, sheep, turkeys, ducks, and chickens. We would need closer to five planet Earths. It simply cannot be done. Free-ranging animals for food can never be more than a specialty market for a few elite buyers.[136]

It seems their solutions are designed to serve only themselves to the exclusion of everyone else, including the animals. Their use of the visibility fictional device seeks to legitimize what would be condemned in the case of cats, dogs, humans, and other animals we value. In the latter cases, witnessing and/or partaking in murder makes you an accessory to the crime or worse. It does not absolve you of wrongdoing.

WASTING

Like visibility, wasting is another common response when we attempt to address the invisibility of farmed animals. Wasting becomes a fictional device when it is used to assert that eating animals is made ethical so long as we don't waste any part of the animal body. There is no disputing the fact that the amount of food we waste is obscene. It's also important to recognize that we only apply the principle of not wasting to the animals we want to eat while excluding it in most other cases. For example, most of us don't go around looking for roadkill or wasted flesh products, dairy, or eggs that stores would otherwise throw out because we feel morally compelled not to waste them. Should we happen to discover abandoned and unfertilized turtle eggs or duck eggs or robin eggs, we do not feel compelled to take them and make a meal out of them so as not to let them go to waste. Notice how we think it's terrible to waste the eggs of chickens by not taking them for our own use, because we assume that they exist for us to eat. But the reason we perceive only chicken eggs as edible, and don't insist on collecting the eggs of other species, is nothing more than cultural conditioning, not a conclusion based on logical or critical thinking. Breeding hens into existence in order to control their bodies and take the eggs that belong to them is a socially acceptable practice, just as slavery was once a socially acceptable practice for millennia up until just a short time ago. Behind the façade of the not-wasting fiction is a deeply entrenched cultural construct that determines who we perceive as *edible*—namely chickens, turkeys, cows, and pigs—versus those who we perceive as *inedible* or even disgusting to eat and therefore exempt from our consideration of wasting—namely all other animals including most wildlife and companion animals.

Examples of the not-wasting fictional device are abundant in popular culture, particularly in more progressive, sustainable, and humane food circles. Urban Adamah claims to kill their chickens after they pass their egg-laying prime (usually just twelve to eighteen months) so that they can provide food for the homeless. The underlying false dilemma in this context can't be overlooked. We claim that we must harm one to help another when in fact we could help both victims, the animals and the homeless, at the same time. Urban Adamah uses the false dilemma as a pretext to kill its chickens instead of supplying the homeless with nutritious plant-based meals, which it could easily do. In spring 2013, Camas Davis, the founder of the Portland Meat Collective, was featured in an editorial in the *New York Times* called "The Proper Way to Eat a Pig," in which she recounts her experience teaching nine high-school-age kids how to slaughter a pig. The article features a striking, stylized photo of her and the kids fashioned after the famous Norman

Rockwell painting of the family sitting around the Thanksgiving table with the turkey as a centerpiece. In the photo, all of the parts of the animal are neatly arranged across the table where the kids are sitting while Davis holds the head of the pig on a shiny silver platter, looking vacuously into the camera. The expression on the pig's face is alive, animated and grinning directly at us, as if he were trying to communicate his pleasure. The photo is so well styled that if you stare at it long enough, it begins to look more and more like a Rockwell painting, steeped in the symbolism of home, community, family, tradition, and American culture—all tied cleverly to the virtue of not wasting and eating the "whole hog." "Once you slaughter a pig, you dehair it, you butcher it, you wrap it and you put it in your freezer, it's so much work you don't want to waste it," says Davis. "It's special."[137] Once again, we see how multiple fictional devices are employed in one story to make it even more powerful.

But is all of this grandiose posturing and Norman Rockwell stylization really about wasting food? If it were truly an issue of wasting, we'd do well to consider the enormous waste of precious resources, like water and land, that raising animals requires. Or how about the fact that about half of the world's edible grain crop is fed to farmed animals instead of the nearly one billion hungry? We should consider the amount of nutritious plant crops that are wasted to feed the animals we eat and how much pollution and climate-changing gases are emitted in that process. If we really cared about conserving rather than wasting the rapidly depleting resources left on this planet, then we are compelled to eat plant foods, eating directly from the source rather than getting our nutrients through an animal, which requires an immense amount of waste and destruction. According to environmental research organization Worldwatch Institute, "it has become apparent that the human appetite for animal flesh is a driving force behind virtually every major category of environmental damage now threatening the human future—deforestation, erosion, fresh water scarcity, air and water pollution, climate change, biodiversity loss, social injustice, the destabilization of communities, and the spread of disease."[138]

Not wasting is also often tied to the anthropomorphic rhetoric of respect for the animal. We claim that the animal, his life and body, was *honored* because his life was not in vain or taken from him in a frivolous manner or for frivolous reasons, but instead with intention, with awareness of the importance of his sacrifice and in the service of the greater good of nourishing us. Again, even if we believed in the anthropomorphic idea that we can pay our respects to animals by paying someone to kill them so we can eat them, we'd still have to admit that the necessity fiction that underlies this idea is absurd. We can easily live without eating animals today. If instead it were actually true that we eat animals today out of necessity, the story might have a legitimate defense, but the troubling fact is that almost any time this idea of respecting the animal by killing and eating him is presented, not only is it not a matter of life and death survival, it's for the most frivolous reason of all: satisfying our taste sensations. A prime example of this fiction can be found in the tagline of the Conscious Carnivore butcher shop, which reads "Respect for every animal, on four feet or two." Its founder, Bartlett Durand, calls himself "the Zen Butcher." The empty call for respect for farmed animals, and then killing them softly, is murder in the case of human beings and other animals we respect and protect from abuse and killing, like our cats and dogs. Since all animals value their lives, killing them unnecessarily is the greatest act of betrayal and disrespect from which there is no recovery. Yes, wasting food is indeed an immense problem, but wasting those who have their whole lives ahead of them for a forgettable meal is even worse.

REDUCTIONISM

Cage-Free But Still Miserable

Food marketers are infamous for using reductionism in their campaigns to fool consumers into believing that a complex problem has a simple solution. Such is the case in the widespread marketing of eggs as "cage-free" and chicken flesh as "free-range." These reductionist tactics are so persuasive that even many of the major animal protection organizations have jumped on the cage-free bandwagon, arguing that a reduction in suffering is better than nothing. The cage-free pitch falsely implies that getting out of cages birds who don't belong in cages to begin with alleviates the problem of using chickens for their eggs, and never is it clearly communicated that cage confinement is just one of numerous sources of suffering associated with exploiting birds for their eggs. The fact that an animal is better off living out of cage confinement is merely stating the obvious, not an attempt to holistically understand the many factors that contribute to their suffering. And what happens once chickens are out of cages but still living in the standard overcrowded squalor on egg farms? Well, like humans forced to live in overcrowded squalor, tensions run high and competition for space, food, and water among individuals and groups of birds is intensified, resulting in pecking, injury, and death. So what's the industry's ingenious solution? Amputate or burn off the tips of the sensitive beaks of newborn chicks to prevent them from pecking at each other, leaving many with painful deformities that make eating difficult or impossible. When the fight to force the egg industry to go cage-free seemed to be in jeopardy, organizations like the Humane Society of the United States (HSUS), with so much vested in this campaign, opted to take reductionism to a whole new level.

In late March 2012, United Egg Producers (UEP) president Gene Gregory made a telling statement at the Annual Conference of the National Institute for Animal Agriculture. Gregory explained his surprise at HSUS's switch from a firm cage-free position to backing the industry's so-called enriched colony cage system and HSUS's willingness to negotiate a deal with UEP on their "new and improved" cage system. The deal essentially boils down to HSUS getting off UEP's back. No more undercover videos exposing the atrocities of egg farms. No more expensive legal battles. No more attacks from the leading animal advocacy organization. And no more state-by-state ballot initiatives that threaten to hurt egg-industry sales. On the contrary, HSUS and other cage-free advocates are applauding agribusiness and food companies for going cage-free, as if cage-free is an end in itself, as if the problem of animal suffering will be solved.

Gregory also described a long history of failed negotiations with HSUS, which he had once referred to as a vegan organization intent on putting the egg industry out of business. The goal of Gregory's statement was to make the case that the new legislation and collaboration with HSUS would phase out battery cages over nearly two decades' time and replace them with the negligibly better enriched colony cages as a way to finally take control of the debate over eggs and animal welfare, and once and for all intercept their biggest threat: the animal advocacy movement. But Gregory's most convincing argument to his audience of skeptical egg farmers was the economic advantage of backing the new deal, citing studies showing that consumers are willing to pay more for "higher welfare" eggs. In other words, he saw the dollar signs and wanted UEP members to see them too. The compromise deal was a win-win situation for HSUS and UEP. Regardless of where one falls on the issue of incremental welfare reform, there is no denying how dilution and reductionism undermined the substance of a legislative battle that was already based on the reductionist logic of getting birds out of cages while ignoring all of the other horrendous practices of the industry. In the end, the overwhelming majority of birds will remain in cages. What's more, sanctuaries and rescuers who have acquired birds from cage-free and enriched colony cage facilities claim that the birds are as bad off or worse than those they've rescued from conventional battery cages. And yet HSUS and others claim that such costly efforts at welfare reform are worth all of the time and effort.

The marketing of free-range poultry products also relies heavily on consumers buying into a reductionist, red-herring ploy. According to United Poultry Concerns, "birds raised for meat may be sold as 'free-range' if they have *government certified* access to the outdoors. The door may be open for only five minutes and the farm still qualifies as 'free-range.' Apart from the 'open door,' no other criteria such as environmental quality, number of birds, or space per bird, are included in the term 'free-range.'"[139] Most chickens raised for flesh products today are technically free-range rather than caged, but they are far from free and certainly not foraging somewhere in an open field or range. Instead, chickens are housed in giant overcrowded sheds, where they are packed in by the thousands and forced to stand and sit on filthy, manure-laden flooring, which is typically cleaned out only every two to four years. In this sense, *free-range* is a meaningless term.[140] But if there is no space to move about in or if birds are trampling on other birds, what benefit could this possibly offer them?

The Slaughterhouse on Wheels

Claiming that slaughter is made humane by bringing the slaughterhouse to the farm or by performing it under carefully controlled conditions (such as kosher and halal methods) is yet another popular form of reductionism being promoted today. This is based on the reductionist logic that the way we treat animals matters but their very lives can be thoughtlessly disposed of in a mere slash of a blade, as long as our intent is to make it as painless as possible for the animal. In June 2013, author Ali Berlow published her book *The Mobile Poultry Slaughterhouse: Building a Humane Chicken-Processing Unit to Strengthen Your Local Food System*, which contains a foreword by Temple Grandin, essentially giving Berlow the official humane movement's seal of approval and legitimacy. Notice how cleverly the title attempts to connect killing chickens as a necessary part of the locavore equation of sustainability, as if killing and sustainability are inevitably connected. In a *Huffington Post* article entitled "Blessed Meat," Berlow invokes the fictional trappings of anthropomorphism to elevate killing to the level of a pious act that honors the animal victims, as if they give a damn what we think as we are about to violently take their lives. Describing her observation of ritual halal slaughter in Africa, she writes, "It was truly blessed meat. Over every animal held in arms and slaughtered, a prayer was said as the swift, sharp deed of taking life in sacrifice was made. There is no denying the gravity of these transforming moments when man, animal, prayer, blade and blood meet. Life is messy and still, all life is holy."[141] Berlow infuses her baroque humane-slaughter fantasy with the visibility fictional devices discussed earlier, suggesting that witnessing this act somehow absolved her of sin.

FEAR

Fear of animals, and the distortion of animal identities as frightful and threatening, seems to be the primary motivator for our detachment from the natural world and other animals in general, and yet notice the conspicuous lack of fear over eating their dead bodies we encounter everyday in neatly wrapped packages. For modern urbanites, the exception is those animals we have domesticated and allowed into our homes. Our fear of farmed animals is paradoxical, considering they are animals whose spirits have been broken by enslavement and the destruction of their natural familial and social order, animals who have been intensively bred to be as subservient and submissive to their human masters as possible. Perhaps our fear is a reaction to the guilt we feel for forcing a life of suffering upon them. It might seem far-fetched to some that deep-seated, irrational fears or phobias about certain species could sanction the mass consumption of still other species, and yet the fictions we are presented with lead us to the false dilemma expressed in phobic statements like "If we don't eat them, they will surely attack or want to eat us"; thus, protecting ourselves seems justifiable. In the Netflix TV show *Zoo*, human characters fear retaliation from animal characters who seek to avenge the wrongs we have perpetrated against them. In Hollywood, this paranoia has roots in epic films like *Jaws*, *Planet of the Apes*, and *The Birds*. In such cases, our notion of vengeance is anthropomorphically projected on to other feared species who we imagine would seek justice, as we would, through violence against their human perpetrators. But there is little evidence for this kind of retaliatory vengeance in other animals. On the contrary, it is remarkable how forgiving nonhuman animals can be, particularly animal survivors of abuse, who knew nothing but callous treatment from humans, yet learned to trust and bond with their new human caretakers. Visiting sanctuaries where turkeys, chickens, cows, and pigs have been given a second chance, it is obvious that the last thing on their minds is vengeance. Our fear of them is truly irrational and fed by the fictions of popular culture.

There is also widespread fear of farmed animals "taking over." The fear that farmed animals would take over if we let them have their way reveals how deftly fear can hijack our ability to think through the facts. Farmed animals would not exist if humans did not artificially breed them into existence in the first place. Our fear of them breeding like crazy and taking over is a fiction we've been fed that eliminates ourselves as the source of the problem—that is, our forced breeding of other animals driven by our demand for animal products. The fear is irrational not only in how it ignores the source of the problem but also in how it imagines a scenario in which billions of animals are suddenly freed from enslavement and allowed to roam and multiply freely. Such an abrupt end to animal exploitation is hardly likely. When the majority of society decides that animal exploitation is inherently wrong, then it is far more likely to see laws that abolish breeding first, perhaps even in phases.

Another form of fictionalized fear is the fearmongering over what could happen to us if we stop eating animals. Our hair will fall out. Our skin will dry up like a prune. Our muscle mass will melt away. Our brains might even shrink! We will become weepy and depressed. In an article published in *Women's Health* called "The Scary Mental Health Risks of Going Meatless"[142] and in Lierre Keith's book *The Vegetarian Myth*, we find classic examples of the backlash that happens whenever a social movement gains a bit of ground and threatens the dominant culture's cozy position of privilege, resulting in personal attacks on the character of the messengers of the cause and dismissing them as "crazy" or "mentally ill."

Chapter 6:

Fictionalizing the Ritual of Consumption

There is a whole set of fictions that ritualize the consumption of animals. They further reinforce the notion that farmed animals are exceptions to animals we should care about. Even for those who aren't convinced by the fictions of denigration, trivialization, fear-mongering, and other assaults on animal identity, there are plenty of fictions that can lure them into eating them anyway. This chapter focuses on the fictions of the animal consumer and the primacy of his interests, no matter how trivial, over the lives of other animals.

TRADITION

Just because something has been done for a very long time is never a valid argument for continuing to do it in the present and the future. And yet, when it comes to defending animal exploitation and consumption, popular culture disseminates a nauseating array of fictions based on tradition. A 2014 SuperValu campaign promoting a line of flesh products shows a life-sized vintage black-and-white photo of a butcher with the brand name placed over his head that reads "Man Cave Craft Meats." Below his feet reads the ad headline, "Long Live the Butcher." Aside from the powerful fictions that associate eating animals with masculinity and strength, the poster taps into another powerful myth about prehistoric man, the long tradition of animal eating and hunting, and the concept of the "man cave" as a narcissistic symbol of the modern male who needs to have his sacred space, independence, and choices respected. Prehistoric humans and their ancestors ate some amount of animal flesh. There's no question about that. However, an in-depth analysis by science writer Rob Dunn published in *Scientific American* reports on recent studies indicating that human ancestors were nearly all vegetarians.[143] But again, is what our ancestors ate relevant to the circumstances we face today regarding our food choices and lifestyles? We are no more compelled to eat like our ancestors than we are to practice cannibalism, rape, slavery, murder, or any of the other violent traditions that are all an unfortunate part of our human legacy.

Urban Adamah: Where "Compassion" and Tradition Collide

Let's consider a case that is supposed to represent the progressive side of our culture, an organization that strives to promote ethics and awareness about our food choices. Urban Adamah, the Jewish organization mentioned in the previous chapter, is an otherwise progressive organization, but it still believes that gratuitously slashing the throats of chickens and goats in an ancient ritual slaughter ceremony is consistent with their mission of compassion. Using chickens as "teaching tools" to help people numb themselves to any emotion as they violently take the lives of animals is cynically pitched as a way for people to get to know where their food comes from.

Consider their arrogance in referring to these lovely young female birds, who are in the prime of their lives yet no longer laying *enough* eggs, as "spent hens," a term coined by the egg industry that defines them in the narrow context of what their reproductive systems can be engineered to produce for them. Can you imagine if we regarded human females as worthless when no longer able to bear children? And can you imagine if we genetically manipulated them without their consent, causing them life-threatening reproductive disorders, cancers, bone fractures, and premature death? Yet this is exactly how Urban Adamah refers to these birds, who, for three years, labored over laying eggs. To add insult to injury, their reward for becoming "spent" is to have their necks slashed while fully conscious by a remorseless kosher slaughterer while another student holds the bird upside down by her ankles and a larger group of students blankly watches over this cultlike murder.

Several media sources predictably defended Urban Adamah's chicken slaughter workshop, comparing it favorably with "factory farming" and criticizing protestors for creating an environment that Adamah claims "would create too much stress for the chickens"[144] during slaughter and which resulted in the cancellation of the workshop. Instead of the chickens being correctly portrayed as the victims, the media framed Urban Adamah as a kind of "puppet victim," while framing those who protested and urged Urban

Adamah to give the chickens up to a sanctuary as the offenders. In the end, Urban Adamah refused those who generously offered their chickens a permanent, loving home and instead killed them in private shortly thereafter, only announcing this after the fact and only after assuring animal advocates that they would not be killed.

If we insist on the importance of perpetuating certain cruel traditions like killing animals for palate pleasure, is this not also an argument in favor of arbitrarily bringing back any of the other insidious traditions that have historically oppressed other "inferior" groups, like women, minorities, gays, and anyone else deemed worthy of inferior treatment? The last (illegal) whaling kill was allowed in the name of tradition by the Makah and was carried out using a not-so-traditional high-powered rifle. The whale bled out for hours before he died. Millions of cows and pigs are shot point blank in the head and billions of chickens and turkeys are plunged into electrified water baths and then have their throats slashed in the name of cultural and traditional eating habits. Since when is violence against the most vulnerable a part of any tradition or culture worth defending?

HISTORY

The status of nonhuman animals changed dramatically some ten thousand to eleven thousand years ago when they became our chattel property and, in many civilizations, even our currency. The advent of what history calls "domestication" is the intensely violent process of capturing and confining animals to a life of unnatural captivity, breeding them for certain traits, controlling reproduction, trafficking offspring, and otherwise bending them to our will in whatever means deemed necessary in order to make them produce something of economic value to us. A 2012 Whole Foods Market branding campaign presented a sheep herder with his flock of sheep in a bucolic, pastoral setting with the campaign tagline inserted below that reads "We Are Earthlings." It's a not-so-subtle metaphor for Jesus Christ, the Good Shepherd, which elevates the small, independent farmer of today to the level of a messiah. Popular culture instills in us a great reverence for traditional farmers who, we are told, farmed animals "the right way." "Animal husbandry," a euphemism for animal exploitation discussed earlier in the book, is perceived as a means for us to reconnect with the land and nature. It seems the more detached and disassociated we urban dwellers become from the natural world, the more precious and rare we regard the traditional farmer, ignoring the fact that our real connection to nature cannot be made through an entirely artificial process of breeding, raising, and slaughtering farmed animals.

Historical accounts of early fur-trading times in the United States refer to wild animals as natural resources just waiting for humans to find them, commodify them, and make a living off of exploiting and killing them. Official history, like the large illustrated plaque in a learning center at the Indiana Dunes National Park, teaches young, impressionable visitors that animals are resources (just like plants and minerals) and exploiting them is part of a noble tradition. They also portray the European settlers as benefiting Native Americans by hiring them to hunt and trap animals exploited for their fur.

In June 2012, *Smithsonian* magazine published a cover story by Jerry Adler and Andrew Lawler called "How the Chicken Conquered the World," which featured an elaborate cover illustration of a chicken with the stature and garb of a royal European monarch. The authors clearly frame their so-called history of the domesticated chicken with an unmistakably anthropocentric bias by opening with these words: "The epic begins 10,000 years ago in an Asian jungle and ends today in kitchens all over the world."[145] It's important to recognize that the Smithsonian is perceived as an authority on history, which essentially means that the widely held opinions expressed here get translated into facts in our mind. From this deranged perspective, the chicken is propped up as the hero who, according to the authors, "saves Western civilization." Forget about the fact that the chicken might be celebrated as a successful species based on the fact that it has survived for thousands of years in its tropical rain forest habitat free of interference from humans. That would be celebrating an animal for his own accomplishments, not ours.

"How the Chicken Conquered the World" is a classic example of another fictional device in which we turn animal victims into false heroes who find themselves used as pawns and trapped in a world in which everything and everyone is defined by their usefulness to us, all so we can stroke our egos and flatter ourselves at how skilled we are at conquering them. Any attempt to understand what they might be experiencing in this context is conveniently ignored in favor of the view we impose upon them, which seeks to legitimize how we want to use them. All this self deception not only strokes our egos, it also helps us overcome any remorse we might feel over all of the harm and suffering we've caused them for so long.

The authors' premise for the article is based on the shoddy assumption that, without chickens and other farmed animals, human civilization could not have prospered and evolved into what it has become today, without citing any credible evidence for what is essentially nothing more than a widely held opinion today. The article ends by trivializing the fate of chickens: "Yes, we get to eat them, but we also feed them." That's one of the earth shattering insights the authors offer us in the closing paragraph of this elaborate piece that seeks to "honor" the chicken.

Historical accounts of the Industrial Revolution credit the Chicago Union Stockyards as a birth place of industrial agriculture. The Yards, as it was known, was the largest meatpacking and slaughtering complex in America for decades, starting in 1865. From the Civil War through the 1920s, more meat was processed in Chicago than in any other place in the world. The district was operated by a group of railroad companies that acquired swampland and turned it into an enormous industrialized hub of animal exploitation. Souvenir postcards from the era show how proudly the city promoted its reputation as "hog butcher to the world." Yet, even then, there were those who sought to expose the ugly truth of their enterprise. Like undercover investigators today, Upton Sinclair spent seven weeks working undercover in Chicago's stockyards before writing his landmark novel, *The Jungle,* using material he had collected firsthand.[146] His intent was to expose the nightmarish conditions of immigrant workers in this environment, but in the process, he also exposed the nightmarish conditions of the animals that were processed through it. While *The Jungle* may have done little to nothing to alleviate animal suffering, it did trigger President Theodore Roosevelt to enact a series of food safety laws shortly thereafter.

PROGRESS

We've seen how major historical milestones were proudly built on the backs of other animals and human slaves, but the same mentality is advanced to commemorate present and future human achievements, with countless self-congratulatory accounts of how miraculously we've mastered the various species we exploit today. In 2004, scientists completed sequencing of the one billion letters in the genome of the red jungle fowl, which is widely believed to be the wild cousin of the domestic chicken. They also identified three million single-letter changes in the chicken genome, known as SNPs, which could be used as markers to search for trait genes.[147] In layperson's terms, the discovery of the chicken genome in 2004 was motivated by a desire to identify specific genes that control the bird's growth and size as well as her egg production. The goal is to improve the *design* of two kinds of chickens: "meat" birds that will grow faster and bigger, and hens that will produce more eggs.

The modern animal-using industries and the scientific-research engine behind them celebrate the biological and genetic manipulation of chickens and other animals for the sole purpose of rendering their eggs, secretions, and flesh into more marketable and profitable commodities. In comparison, the only permissible form of genetic manipulation of humans—which remains controversial—is for life-saving medical advancements. Their rhetoric of exploitation is based on two key messages that are incessantly repeated: First, their use of animals is a win-win situation, beneficial to the animals and us. Second, technological innovations in animal science serve the greater good by feeding the world's growing population. We boast about how we can accelerate the growth of a baby "broiler" chick into an adult body in just forty-two days and force a cow to produce up to twelve times more milk than her body would normally yield to feed just one calf and force a hen to lay up to three hundred eggs per year. According to the Penn State College of Agricultural Sciences website, "the modern broiler industry has developed a hybrid that is unlike any other breed. . . . Today's broiler can achieve a 5-pound market weight in five weeks. These advances are the result of scientific progress in genetic, nutritional, and environmental research."[148] Note how they use the word *hybrid* as if they're discussing a Prius—which incidentally ties in to the objectification fictional device we covered earlier. But even the word *broiler* is suspect. Is it euphemistic to call a bird a "broiler"? Not necessarily. It's just a complete annihilation of the living bird in favor of how his corpse will be used, a reference to the processed, cooked, and prepared body parts on our plate.

In another section of the Penn site, they describe the miracle of modern chicken breeding as a *natural* phenomenon: "The parent breeders are the birds that produce the fertile eggs that will become the broiler chickens that are harvested for meat. Breeders are raised in open floor houses with automatic watering, feeding, and egg collection systems. Males and females are allowed to mate naturally. Females begin producing eggs around 24 weeks of age and will lay efficiently for 40 weeks per cycle."[149] Note the strategic use of euphemisms here. *Harvesting* replaces *slaughtering. Mate naturally* is used to describe the unnatural, horrible, and confined conditions under which females have no chance of escaping male attacks. The conditions are not just unnatural; they are completely controlled in terms of lighting, ambient temperature, flooring, confinement, feeding, social interaction, drugs, mutilations, and other painful procedures. In fact, as one delves into the industry's literature, the environmental controls are considered critical to productive and profitable breeding. "Open floor houses" are nothing more than barren warehouses with cement flooring covered in shavings that become wet with feces and full of pathogens, upon which thousands of birds are forced to live in typically crowded quarters.

Wall Street Journal columnist Matt Ridley praises the alleged advances of the poultry industry in a 2011 article he entitled "Reasons to Crow About Ever-Bigger Chickens." Ridley touts all of this intensive manipulation of birds as "the power of selection," a reference to the advances in the genetic manipulation and breeding of chickens since the 1950s, which sounds strikingly similar to the Nazi eugenics programs of the fascist era. While Ridley comes off sounding like an agribusiness talking head, he ends with a curious recognition that the suffering of chickens might actually need to be addressed, if ever so flippantly: "Nor is it clear that their [chickens] living one-third as long is any crueler, since they are killed either way — and they can be bred to be less fretful."[150] It's a dishonest attempt to justify killing someone at a fraction of their natural life span. We're all going to die anyway. Does that mean it is justifiable to kill infants since they might otherwise die of natural causes instead? And what about the fact that none of this is even necessary? If suffering is inflicted unnecessarily, is it not inherently cruel by virtue of being unnecessary?

All of this industry rhetoric of progress is strategically channeled through the marketing departments of animal-industry titans like ConAgra and Tyson, which fabricate one clever and creative execution after another targeted at their young audience. The chick-hatching exhibit at the Museum of Science and Industry in Chicago has been operating since the 1950s as part of its Genetics exhibit. Here, starry-eyed children are dazzled by the high-tech-looking displays and the "future of medicine and food" messaging, and are wooed by adorable baby chicks struggling to break through their shells. All the while, this controlled environment hides the violence and cruelty at the core of decades of selective and genetic manipulation and animal testing. What's worse, a 1998 investigation by United Poultry Concerns uncovered the fact that the thousands of baby chicks that are hatched each year at the museum end up at the Lincoln Park Zoo. When UPC wrote to the zoo to inquire about what happens to these chicks, the general curator wrote back, stating that "while some chicks received at Lincoln Park Zoo become participants in educational programs, most are utilized as nutrition for reptiles in the collection." What this essentially means is that the chicks are gassed and suffocated and turned into fodder.

Another form of fictionalized progress comes from the animal welfare movement, where major milestones and victories are declared for what often mean little or no relief from suffering for the animals themselves. Welfarism relies on fictionalized consent—the idea that animals don't mind being used so it's just a matter of how we treat them—as well as reductionism, whereby a complex problem is reduced to a simple solution. The result is single-minded marketing slogans like "free-range" or "cage-free" that imply that our ethical obligation to animals is met by making a single improvement to their lives, which, in reality, are filled with a multitude of sources of suffering and frustration. The more cynical form of welfarism comes from animal-industry science itself which experiments on "broiler" chickens to see if intentionally breeding them blind would make them less distressed on farms, or if removing their cerebral cortex—thereby rending them brain-dead—would make them insensate to suffering. "What if the chicken's brain could be scientifically expunged?," asks Karen Davis of United Poultry Concerns. "What if the elements of memory, instinct, sensation and emotion could be eliminated and a brainless chicken constructed?"[151] Is this the kind of future shock scenario where welfarism and progress intersect? To some extent, the future is now. In the United Kingdom, an architecture student named Andre Ford has proposed what he calls the "Headless Chicken Solution" to the suffering of chickens on factory farms.[152]

EVOLUTION

There are two main categories of evolutionary fictions. The first category claims that farmed animals have been bred and used by humans for food for so long that they have somehow evolved into this role of feeding us, which is another way of saying that they are consensual because they've gotten used to being treated as chattel property. Arguments defending human slavery and exploitation often follow the same logic, claiming that the freedom of those who have fought for and earned freedom is only possible when other, "lesser" people are enslaved, as in the case of institutionalized slavery dating back to ancient Rome.[153] Similarly, the main defense of the exploitation of modern-day sweatshop laborers is based on what we call the fallacy of relative privation,[154] in which the victims don't know anything better than exploitative treatment anyway, and even if they did, their exploiters offer them an overall better life than their other options.

The second category of fictions claims that the human body has evolved from a long history of eating animals, which is consequently the basis for our dietary needs today. In other words, to use a clever expression from author Charles Horn, "evolution has a gun to our heads to eat animals."[155] In still other arguments, eating animals is the reason why we have evolved into such a supreme species endowed with such big brains. Conversely, evolution is typically dismissed as "just a theory" when animal advocates cite the fact that the advent of Darwinism and evolutionary science dispels the myth of human exceptionalism, of the "us and them" mentality. Instead, Darwin demonstrated how we all share a common ancestry, which represented a paradigm shift in thinking from millennia of religious doctrine that preached human dominion over other animals. If evolution is just a theory, then creationism and intelligent design are "just theories" too, and since they are based on faith rather than empirical inquiry, they present a far weaker and more subjective ideological basis for causing animals to suffer. And if we are going to cause mass suffering, shouldn't we be damn sure we're doing it for some good reason, rather than on a leap of faith?

The Fictional Food Chain

Claiming to be at the top of the food chain is an affirmation of our ability to violently dominate everything and everyone and is based on the principle of "might makes right," which is responsible for the worst atrocities and crimes against humanity and other animals. According to several French researchers, as people become wealthier, they tend to eat more meat and fewer plant foods.[156] Wealth, status, and privilege are associated with eating more animals and the belief that we are at the "top of the food chain." This association has led to massive increases in meat consumption in many developing countries including China, India, Brazil, and South Africa.

Those who believe there is scientific basis for the claim that humans are at the top of the food chain should consider that, in 2013, for the first time ever, scientists used a statistical method of calculating a species's trophic level (its level or rank in a food chain) based on its diet. Their findings, published in the *Proceedings of the Natural Academy of Sciences*,[157] scored humans at 2.21 on a scale of one to five, roughly equal to an anchovy or a pig. On the low end of the scale are primary producers like plants, and on the higher end are pure apex predators (animals that eat only meat and have few or no predators of their own, such as tigers, crocodiles, or boa constrictors). Unfortunately, this study doesn't look critically at the fact that belonging to a food chain implies that modern humans are living in the natural world as subsistence hunter-gatherers, competing with other species for food, as if our only choices are based on what we can find and hunt. In other words, it ignores the important moral distinction that comes from our ability to choose from a wide variety of food options, in contrast to other animals in the wild who have no choice but to eat what is available to them.

We humans are not at the top of anything. We are merely part of an interdependent web of life that forms complex yet fragile ecosystems. We choose to either participate in the protection of these natural systems or to destroy them, at our own peril. The concept of a food chain is a human construct that imposes a rigid and competitive hierarchy among species, rather than a good faith understanding of the complexity of the ecosystems to which we belong. Using our power of choice, rather than relying on a theory of biological determinism that favors eating animals, we choose plant foods to get all the nutrients we need through primary sources of nourishment, in the most ecological and resource-efficient manner possible, thereby minimizing our harm to other animals, humans, and the planet.

Big-Brain Theories

Another popular evolutionary fiction is based on the assertion that our brains developed from eating animals. Well, our brains have also evolved to become addicted to smoking, gambling, video games, alcohol, drugs, sex, violence, and harmful fast food. Our brains have evolved to create complex societies led by Hitlers and Stalins along with great visionaries like Gandhi and Leonardo da Vinci. Fortunately, our brains appear to also be well equipped at making rational and moral judgments about what is good and bad, what is right and wrong—for ourselves and for others directly affected by our decisions. And we recognize that just because we are endowed with the capacity for something doesn't necessarily mean we should use it. We've evolved into an age where our weapons of mass destruction could annihilate all life on this planet, but it would be madness to try to justify using them based on the fact that we had the mental capacities to develop them!

Often referred to as the expensive tissue hypothesis, the widely accepted claim that our brain size and complexity are connected to eating animals has been rigorously tested and refuted in a key report published in *Nature*. This comprehensive report evaluates the research into more than one hundred mammalian species, including twenty-three primate species, analyzing brain size and organ-mass data. Lead researcher Ana Navarrete concludes that "human encephalization [brain development] was made possible by a combination of stabilization of energy inputs and a redirection of energy from locomotion, growth and reproduction."[158] But even if the expensive tissue hypothesis were true, would it really matter? Just as the fact that our country was built by slaves does not justify the continued enslavement of other human beings, neither would the fact that our brain size evolved from eating animals be a justification for continuing to exploit animals for food when we have no need to do so.

Lesley Rogers, professor emeritus of neuroscience at University of New England, has made outstanding contributions to understanding brain development and behavior. She discovered lateralization in the chick forebrain.[159] Prior to Rogers's discovery, it was widely accepted that only humans and certain primates had lateralized brains, which endow us with "multitasking" and advanced cognitive states. Later it became known that hemispheric specialization is ubiquitous in the animal kingdom. It's important to recognize that the study of neuroscience and brain function is in its infancy. The truth is we still have much to learn about the brains of other animals as well as our own.

NEUTRALITY

One popular, pseudointellectual idea today is that moral relativity arises logically from the evolutionary and scientific worldview. Neutrality becomes fiction when behavior that is condemned when humans are the victims becomes acceptable when other animals are the victims. Framing the issue of animal exploitation and suffering as a matter of opinion is yet another way animal victims are neutralized. In response to criticism from animal advocates, Brock Peterson, a major stakeholder in Pig Adventure (a kind of pig factory farm open to the public) told the press, "Some people who don't like to eat meat or don't want others to eat meat think all animal production processes are cruel in and of themselves and we respect their opinion."[160] Pig Adventure opened to the public in August 2013 with the goal of unapologetically putting industrial pig farming on display. On the surface, Peterson's statement sounds reasonable and diplomatic, but it's actually a common trivialization tactic. The same tactics were used to trivialize other injustices, including slavery, rape, and racism. The tactic consists of denying that the inferior group counts morally and therefore has no serious interests to protect. And even if they did have interests, ending their exploitation would cause some unacceptable harm to the "greater good."

Neutrality is often invoked in response to stating that harming animals is wrong. This neutrality can be expressed through such statements as "I'm not *for* animal abuse, but then I don't see the problem or oppose animals being killed for food." But since when do we consider someone who benefits from the victimization of others to be a credible source of moral judgment? Claiming that you *don't mind* if others suffer is a dishonest statement made from a position of human privilege, much like male privilege or white privilege, which ignores or trivializes the victim. Whether we choose to recognize it, the reality of the victim's suffering still exists for them. Regardless of what we think, farmed animals communicate their anxiety, fear, pain, trauma, loss, and despair through body language and vocalizations. They will fight like hell for their lives and the lives of their offspring.

Finally, neutrality is often implied when we invoke "freedom of choice," as if there were no one harmed by our choice to eat animal products, as if the actions we take as free agents are exempt from moral scrutiny. But this is just a fiction we tell ourselves that ignores how we violate the freedom of others in attaining our own.

JUDGMENT

Related to holding a position of neutrality is our aversion to passing judgment and our call for nonjudgment when it comes to the food choices we make. Even when we are making judgments about bad ideas, like eating animals for no good reason, that are not directed at specific individuals or groups, many are personally offended by judging a practice or idea as immoral. They mistakenly view the judgment we make to defend animals as a form of bigotry. But there is a hidden judgment in the statement "Don't judge . . ." If we claim that others should not be judged for eating animal products, then we also make the judgment that an animal's entire lifetime of experiences is worth even less than satisfying some trivial, momentary taste sensation. Such a judgment stems from an entrenched prejudice against a handful of species that we just so happen to want to exploit and kill for food. Once we become aware of this prejudice—and the ensuing injustice perpetrated against its victims—there is no personal, neutral, or morally relative position on eating animal products, especially since we have no biological need to eat them. If animals matter even in the most superfluous sense, then we don't violate their most basic right to life and liberty when we can easily avoid it, such as in the case of replacing animal products with alternatives.

There is a rare yet powerful indictment of our moral neutrality over animal suffering in the popular television drama *Breaking Bad*, where character Jesse Pinkman attends a drug rehab support group and confesses to killing a dog for apparently no good reason (in truth, it's a man, not a dog, he has killed). The social worker moderating the group asks, "How did you feel about what you did, Jesse?"

> Support group woman (interjecting): Who cares how you feel! What kind of a person kills a dog for no reason? . . . You don't just sit there and talk about killing a helpless, innocent animal —
>
> Social worker (interrupting): We're not here to sit in judgment.
>
> Jesse (tearful but defiant): Why not? Maybe she's right. . . . Maybe I should have done something different. The thing is, if you just do stuff and nothing happens, what's it all mean? What's the point? . . .
>
> Social worker: Kicking the hell out of yourself doesn't give meaning to anything.

Jesse: So I should stop judging and accept? So no matter what I do, hurray for me because I'm a great guy? It's all good? No matter how many dogs I kill I just, what, do an inventory and accept? I mean you back your truck over your own kid and you, like, accept? What a load of crap![161]

As a moral anchor in a sea of depravity, Jesse rejects the self-serving moral relativism of "don't judge" and accepts that his actions have consequences for others, that innocent victims matter.

IMPOSSIBILITY

While neutrality denies that we are obligated to defend animals, impossibility is used as a fictional device by imposing impossible standards and criteria for granting animals access to our exclusive morality club. We have a wide range of reasons why it is impossible for animals to have lives that matter to them more than our taste buds matter to us, why it is impossible for us not to exploit them or pay someone else to exploit them to satisfy our taste sensations, and why it is impossible for society to change from accepting the current abhorrent treatment and use of animals to rejecting this. We claim that unless farmed animals can be perfect and saint-like in their actions, they deserve to be killed and eaten. Or, we say, when animals can talk, reason, solve mathematical problems, build skyscrapers, send a man to the moon, paint a Rembrandt, or do whatever it is that we think makes humans so exceptional and unique, we'll continue to pay someone to kill animals so we can eat them. That's the meathead logic we use for causing such immense suffering to farmed animals. With other animals, we cut them more slack, never claiming that bad behavior is grounds for killing and eating them. We're not consistent among species.

"I'll stop eating meat when a cow can get me out of prison."[162] That was a line from an episode of *Orange Is the New Black* in which one inmate responds to another inmate who announces she is vegetarian. Of course, the vegetarian character is the same one that everyone loves to ridicule. You can't have a likable vegetarian character in popular culture. Instead, we must fashion her into the shallow, negative stereotype of the pious vegetarian. Popular culture must stigmatize, discriminate against, and marginalize vegetarian characters to pander to the dominant meat-eating audience and give them ample grounds to dismiss them. To stop eating meat when a cow can get me out of prison, to employ the impossibility fiction, is not unlike the logic of the PhD professor/journalist in *New Scientist* who recently wrote that a lion can't have the right not to be hunted, killed, and eaten unless he can commit to not killing another human. In other words, I'll stop harming you when you can meet my one impossible condition.

PURITY
Self-Sufficiency as Moral Purity
Some go well beyond shopping for humane labels in the store and advocate for complete self-sufficiency, revealed in common statements like "I only eat eggs from my neighbor's backyard hens" or "We only eat the animals we hunt or find on the side of the road." It's part of the "living off the grid" fantasy that demands total self-sufficiency and conscientious objection to our food system, a lifestyle precious few on our planet could ever come close to achieving. And the corporate food marketing engine is already wise to it. Take, for example, Whole Foods Market, which sells eggs that claim to be pasture raised from backyard hens and paleo granola that sells for $12.99/lb.

Even if this were a more-easily-attainable goal, looking for rare situations where it could be considered ethical to eat the eggs of chickens or the flesh of animals is a misguided fixation that misses the point and distracts us from the big picture, which is that we cause an enormous amount of suffering to animals by supporting the industry that breeds and hatches them, regardless of how well we treat them. To meet consumer demand for eggs, every year we kill six billion male chicks globally,[163] and in the United States alone we slaughter 280 million twelve- to eighteen-month-old juvenile hens when they out-live their egg-laying prime, while confining most of them to cages.[164] And even those "lucky" hens who are allowed to live out their lives in someone's backyard are prisoners in their own bodies; they cannot control the obscenely unnatural quantity of eggs they lay (thanks to our manipulation of their reproduction) and therefore are susceptible to painful complications due to egg laying and premature death.[165] If we have a genuine interest in helping these birds, the least we can do for them is to challenge and overcome our bizarre fixation on their eggs and our egg-industry prejudice about them as "egg layers." In fact, if we did not burden them with egg laying, they would be busy doing many other things in life. If we can get over our fixation with their eggs, we will not become morally "pure" or "perfect," but we might just discover what rich and complex lives they lead.

Moral purity through self-sufficiency is not limited to egg consumption. The idea that there is moral purity or superiority in killing the meat you eat (as opposed to paying someone else to do the dirty work for you) is often connected to a highly romanti-cized and unrealistic vision of how traditional or indigenous people live and find their food. Films like *Into the Wild* and TV shows like *Survivor* and *Lost* popularize and pander to this fantasy of ours, targeting an apparently bored upper-middle-class audience looking for a sense of adventure. The harsh reality is that climate change has already made certain regions of the world inhospita-ble to both raising livestock and cultivating food crops, and the trend will increase, forcing these populations to obtain food from outside sources. Two examples are the Mongolians and the Inuit. Like Mongolians, the Inuit practice of hunting on ice has been decimated by climate change. Unlike Mongolians, Inuit don't have fields suitable to grow food for all their meals. Yet that just makes them the same as most urban and suburban dwellers. In fact, Inuit today generally no longer live in igloos, but rather in modern com-munities with modern building structures and municipalities. The Inuit can and already do, in fact, buy food grown elsewhere.

Misrepresenting Veganism as Moral Purity

Sometimes purity has very positive connotations in our culture. Other times it is associated with just being strange, eccentric, or crazy and therefore easily dismissed. In the innovative HBO television series *Six Feet Under*, Nate's old girlfriend and soon-to-be-wife, Lisa, is introduced in the story as a likeable, if not somewhat predictable, granola-crunching vegan stereotype, but things quickly decline into absurdity, ensuring that any real or positive influence she might have as the lone vegan character in a nonvegan drama is obliterated. In one scene, Claire walks in to her kitchen to find Lisa on the floor talking to the ants who have invaded her home. She explains to Claire that she is "communicating" with the ants to nicely ask them to leave her house. Later that evening in a scene at the dinner table, Lisa serves Nate and Claire a tofu dish, which they can barely eat because it's apparently so inedible, further reinforcing just how strange and unsatisfying being a vegan must be. But the icing on the cake comes when Lisa explains how she won't go to the movies since film is processed with gelatin from animal hooves and therefore contributes to the global slavery of animals. But the story leaves out the important fact that gelatin only exists as a by-product of slaughterhouses, which only exist because of our demand for eggs, dairy, and flesh products.

What HBO and the character Lisa tragically reveal is that popular culture has rarely if ever developed a believable, let alone influential or engaging, vegan character up to now because it just might get us thinking that we could relate to them too much. HBO, from which we have come to expect more cutting-edge programming, leads us into the same tired and outdated fictional traps, portraying veganism as a state of moral purity or extremism, not unlike the worst examples from tabloid television. It's a disappointing shortcoming of the writers of an otherwise highly creative drama. Later in the series, when Lisa ends up marrying Nate and has their baby, she is seen shopping for and eating animal products, suddenly betraying her vegan diet for no apparent reason or explanation. It's assumed that perhaps, since she is a nursing mother, she needs animal products again? But even the Academy of Nutrition and Dietetics, which typically takes a conservative and sometimes even antagonistic position on vegetarianism, nonetheless clearly states that a vegan diet can be healthful in any stage of a person's life, including nursing mothers.[166]

The idea that not eating eggs, dairy, and flesh, or replacing them with something even more nutritious, is some kind of moral or philosophical purity is one of the most damaging vegan fictions, and one that has become all too often reinforced by vegans themselves. Misrepresenting veganism as something more remote and utopian than it really is only reinforces the outdated notion that it *is* remote and utopian, rather than a simple act of reaching for one product over another on the store shelf. Veganism is as accessible in practice as it is on principle—a rejection of animal exploitation—for the same reasons we reject human exploitation, which has no more to do with purity or perfection than does the same rejection of human exploitation.

One of the negative consequences of the dissemination of this powerful fiction of vegan purity or perfection is the rise of a population of "almost-vegans" who are languishing on the threshold. So what is it that keeps them from making the seemingly small step to "come out" as a proud vegan who then becomes a role model for others? As long as people associate veganism with perfection or purity, imperfect and impure beings as we are, identifying and committing to veganism as a way of life will seem unnecessary and extreme, rather than a powerful strategy for changing the world for animals. The almost-vegans will therefore continue to appease both our vegan friends on the one hand and our nonvegan friends on the other, allowing animal-eating social norms to sabotage their sense of right and wrong.

Another factor in getting past the perfection fiction could be letting go of all the cultural indoctrination to which we've been subjected all of our lives. Some of us are physical hoarders, but others are psychological hoarders, still hanging on to certain beliefs and norms that perhaps make them feel personally and socially more secure. Ingrained notions of health, familial ties, social or cultural rituals, and fragments of our personal identity can all be tied to certain animal foods. The almost-vegan fears the social pressures and stigmas associated with not eating animals and wants to fit in. But the moral dilemma we must all ultimately face is whether it is worth abandoning our fundamental belief that animals should not be violated to serve human pleasures in order to conform or avoid conflict when we know and accept there is a victim in that decision, when we know that the consequences of doing so are literally a matter of life and death. Again, we do not become pure or perfect simply because we recognize and act on this reality.

Masculinity

It would not be difficult to fill this whole book with examples from popular culture of how masculinity is used as a fictional device to condition both men and women to eat more animals. Beyond these ubiquitous examples from our everyday lives, we can also turn to high-level research studies that give us more formal evidence of the power of the meat-masculinity connection. One such high-profile study published by the *Journal of Consumer Research* entitled "Is Meat Male?"[167] sets out to demonstrate the various ways in which meat serves as a metaphor for masculinity that can impact a wide variety of consumer preferences, from shoes to cars, power tools, food, and beyond. At least in part, the study is intended to provide brand managers with new quantitative research to better understand how meat is positively associated with masculinity in Western cultures on a variety of levels and what psychological factors distinguish "brand champions" from potential "brand switchers." Yet these metaphors manifest themselves far beyond the world of brands and deep into the recesses of popular cultural consciousness.

Some might be surprised to see the meat-masculinity fiction featuring female protagonists and targeted to a female audience, but indeed it is not exclusively reserved for the domain of the male consumer. "Conquer one cut of meat at a time" is the main message of Target's 2014 TV commercial featuring a stylish young woman playing the role of a matador (traditionally a male role in Spanish culture), suggesting that the path to becoming a powerful woman means taking on traditional, patriarchal roles of ritual violence and domination over animals. It's interesting to see how American brands like Target continue to perpetuate violent and cruel traditions like bullfighting even while the tide appears to be turning in Spain itself, where opposition to bullfighting has strengthened. To maintain its appeal to traditional feminine symbols, the whole ad is whitewashed, conveying qualities like chastity, purity, and freshness, helping us further disassociate from the bloody mess of slaughter.

In the film *Rocky,* the scene of fighter Rocky Balboa in the slaughterhouse using a hanging animal carcass as a punching bag symbolizes human supremacy and brutality over other animals, a morbid hypermasculinity, and our fight to the "top of the food chain."[168] Beating the slaughtered and dismembered animal is associated with the rise of a true champion, affirming the role of violence in traditional conceptions of masculinity. Powerful images such as this one shape our culture's widely held and unfounded beliefs about meat, protein, strength, health, and masculinity, often on a subconscious or subliminal level. Similarly, the 2015 Nissan Rogue "Bull Chase" TV commercial features a handsome and stylish young couple zipping through a labyrinth of winding streets in a historic European city center where they are surrounded by bulls, some running beside their car and others confronting them head on around turns. Eventually, they open into a piazza where they park in front of the Toro Steakhouse. The young man gets out of the car and sees a bull in front of him and gives him the look of victory. The bull snorts and backs off. And the couple enters the steakhouse. The message is that consumption is the ultimate act of conquest over other animals. The commercial closes with the "Choose Nissan" logo searing into the white background with a hot metal branding iron. As with Rocky, beating the animal at his own game is a rite of passage to an evolved male identity.

In the Starz television series *Magic City*, the character Ben Diamond breaks new ground. Unlike in *Rocky*, instead of meat being associated with traits like strength and masculinity, it is associated with our basest instincts. Diamond grew up in a Jewish orphanage and now functions as an adult sociopath, destroying one life after another in his pursuit of riches. He describes himself as so ruthless in the slaughterhouse where he worked as a young man that he became nicknamed "the Butcher." The story makes a clear connection between sadism and violence against human and other animal victims.

In a scene from season five of *Six Feet Under*, Nate, and Brenda are having a dinner party and a bird gets into their kitchen because they left a window open. They coax him out but the bird finds his way back in the house again. This time Brenda cries out for Nate's help (as if she and the other women in the room are incapable of handling the situation), and he comes in and kills the bird by attacking him with a broom. No one objects. All of the strong female characters in the series, and several of the male characters— one who used to be a cop and another who is a biology professor who reveres nature—just sit back and watch the assault on the bird. They express regret but no objection, reinforcing the "damsel in distress" female stereotype as well as the violent-male stereotype embodied in the character Nate, who acts out aggressively even when there is no real threat. Strangely, as with hunters, this all gets twisted into some idea of the male protector/provider of the family.

Male privilege in the branding of animal agriculture is inextricably tied to the fact that the industry relies on the total control and systematic violation of the reproductive organs of female animals. Even as USDA census data show more women in agriculture (30 percent as of 2007),[169] the industry's communications appeal overwhelmingly to Caucasian men and are steeped in misogyny. "If she can't stay pregnant, what will she do?" reads the headline in a series of ads for a bovine pharmaceutical product called Bovi-Shield HB by Pfizer Animal Health. In one execution of the ad, a handsome, fifty-something Caucasian male who is supposed to represent a farmer (but is undoubtedly a paid model) kneels down in front of the camera with a hunting rifle propped up on his side and the dead pheasants he's shot laid out in front of him. His dairy cow holds a pheasant in her mouth. The scene suggests that the cow isn't producing milk for him and so he's found another way to have her earn her keep by facetiously taking on the role of a hunting dog. The ad captures the mentality of animal agriculture where female animals are powerless, bred and exploited for the very traits that render them servile and submissive to men. Their value is defined by their reproductive output, which, consequently, is the way the industry names them: "egg layers," "milk producers," and "baby machines."

Female animals are repeatedly and forcibly impregnated, causing untold physical and psychological distress. In the dairy industry, farm workers shove one arm up a dairy cow's rectum and, with the other arm, insert a probe into her vagina, looking at a computer monitor to determine when would be the "optimal" time to impregnate her, while her head is locked in a restraint or her entire body in a constraining device the industry refers to as a "rape rack." In any other context, this act would be considered sexual assault, rape, or bestiality. But when the same act is performed routinely, it's suddenly acceptable. In the words of critical animal studies author Carmen M. Cusack, "the law permits animal husbandry as an exception/defense to sexual contact with and hence abuse of animals. This exception/defense recognizes that animal husbandry violates animals sexually, e.g. requires cows to be raped, which is penetration without consent. However, husbandry is treated as exception/defense because it is 'accepted' by the farming industry."[170] Female animals toil through pregnancies and give birth only to have their offspring taken from them. When masculinity is used as a fictional device, it is the female animals' duty and honor to serve the men who own them.

DISTRACTION

At the core of this discussion about eating animals is an undeniable truth: we don't *need* to artificially breed, raise, and kill animals for food, fashion, entertainment, education, etc., especially when faced with the abundance of alternatives. We only do it because we can get away with silencing the victims and concealing their suffering. We can also send a man to the moon and apply our technological prowess to any challenge. Solutions appear swiftly and society adapts to them, sometimes without even realizing any change has occurred. When it comes to the immense scale of gratuitous suffering we cause animals, we use distraction as a fictional device to outright ignore or deflect attention away from two important facts: First, we are technologically advanced enough to render eating animals obsolete. Sociologist Victoria Johnson writes, "For the first time in history, we have the opportunity through technological innovation to eliminate the human/animal caste system, together with its rituals of 'natural' superiority and inferiority that continue to underpin sexist, racist, classist, and other forms of stratification in the present."[171] Second, the abundance of alternatives are already staring most of us in the face, wherever our eyes land on the supermarket shelf or on the menu in the restaurant or at the office cafeteria. It's becoming increasingly difficult to ignore the growing market for animal-free products. Yet denial persists, often expressed in the form of distraction—shifting focus off of the issue at hand and on to something else in an attempt to avoid what has psychologically pained us throughout history. But we could easily liberate ourselves from that painful dilemma, since the dilemma has vanished. We can choose plant foods.

Eating Animals to Save Them?

One popular form of distraction for avoiding the fact that we don't need to eat animals is by shifting the focus onto vegans and veganism. In the last several years, a few academic studies and an onslaught of pseudoscientific arguments in favor of eating pasture-raised animals have gained in popularity primarily in the so-called sustainable, progressive food movement, claiming that if vegans factor in the amount of animal deaths resulting from the harvesting of plant crops, they would find that vegan and vegetarian diets result in a greater number of animal deaths than diets based on pasture-raised animals. In essence they challenge the vegan position that a diet free of animal products minimizes harm to animals.

On the scholarly front is professor Steven Davis of Oregon State University, who published a well-known paper on the subject in which he poses the question "Is it possible that some other agricultural production alternatives may result in least harm to animals?" going on to conclude that "the least harm principle may actually be better served using food production systems that include both plant-based agriculture and a forage-ruminant-based agriculture as compared to a strict plant-based (vegan) system."[172] Davis's theory quickly gained a locavore following eager for some scientific validation of their desire to eat pasture-raised animals. Some call this the "kill what you eat" movement widely found in major media op eds, independent blogs, and social media.

One recent example is a *New York Times* op ed by Kate Murphy called "Blessed Be My Freshly Slaughtered Dinner."[173] Murphy turns a sympathetic eye on a trend she claims began about five years ago but reached an important milestone with Facebook founder Mark Zuckerberg's announcement that he would eat meat only from animals he killed himself (even though, according to the article, he ended up paying someone else to do the dirty work for him). Murphy captures the spirit of a movement that praises the virtues of taking responsibility for your food choices and becoming more self-reliant as a form of conscientious objection to Big Food. Attracted to this movement are hunters, foragers, paleos, and anyone else seeking to emulate a life "off of the grid" and "back to the land." Murphy even makes a halfhearted acknowledgment of animal ethics by quoting Ingrid Newkirk, president of People for the Ethical Treatment of Animals, who she claims "predictably" opposes the unnecessary killing of animals. "Those within the eat-what-you-kill community," Murphy writes, "respond [to the vegan opposition] that it's no more empathetic to eat a plant-based diet when so many animals are routinely snared, shot or incidentally shredded in crop cultivation. Moreover, hunters argue that they have greater empathy because they must put themselves in the mind of the animal to understand its volitions and desires to predict its movements and reactions."[174] But the comprehensive and well-researched study "Number of Animals Killed to Produce One Million Calories in Eight Food Categories," published by AnimalVisuals's Mark Middleton, reveals a very different reality as well as the many flaws in Steven Davis's analysis. Middleton concludes that "a diet that includes animal products will result in more animal deaths than a plant-based diet with the same number of calories" and that "the most animal suffering and death can be prevented by following a vegan diet."[175]

Intention is an important ethical consideration in assessing the culpability of an act. The unintentional killing of field mice and other animals during the process of harvesting essential food crops is a vastly different scenario from one in which billions of sentient individuals are deliberately and artificially bred into existence for the sole purpose of exploiting and killing them for flesh and secretions that are unnecessary for our health. Professor Gary Francione calls this "a version of the argument that if we cannot avoid unintentional death, we might as well engage in intentional killing." Francione asks us to imagine what the reaction would be if it were human lives at stake instead: "Think about that. We cannot avoid accidental or unintended death in manufacturing anything, including the most innocuous and beneficial of products. So it's okay to kill humans intentionally? Surely not."[176]

Still, many crop farmers intentionally kill what they consider pest animals that threaten their crops, but animal farmers kill even more to protect their herds and flocks as well as the feed they must purchase to sustain them. Also, nonlethal, humane solutions to crop protection do exist and with growing consumer awareness and demand could drive their adoption by farmers. As Francione points out, "If we were all vegans and embraced the moral personhood of nonhumans, we would undoubtedly devise better ways of avoiding even incidental and unintended deaths of animals in the crop production process."[177] In the end, the notion that killing what you eat makes you ethically superior to those who don't is nothing more than invoking the principle of might makes right. And might makes right rules out any serious consideration of the least-harm principle.

An example of how this works in the consumer-centered world of popular culture is Patagonia, which ironically has a reputation for being a forward-thinking brand. Yet its Traceable Down program appears to be more about pandering to barbaric traditions than promoting a saner, more sustainable future. Compared to conventional methods of down production, Patagonia claims to provide consumers with an ethical alternative. As a Patagonia representative explained in an e-mail dated November 7, 2014, "the Traceable Down Standard, developed by Patagonia, ensures that every down cluster in every down product can be traced back to birds that were never force-fed and never live-plucked. So customers can be assured that our down has not been mixed in the process."

Their clever promotional video disassociates Patagonia from the immensely cruel standard practices for procuring down while ignoring the gravest moral transgression of all: the mass slaughter of baby birds necessary to procure the raw materials for their products. The video uses subterfuge to mask the violence and killing of four-month-old baby birds by focusing our attention instead on the claim that these birds were never live plucked or force fed. They employ the humane meat fallacy, which claims that the way animals are treated during the short time they are allowed to stay alive matters, but their very lives are worth nothing and are therefore easily disposable and replaceable. A whole lifetime of experiences can be destroyed in an instant with no ethical consideration, all in the name of fashion and profit. Patagonia tells us the baby birds will be slaughtered anyway for meat, so why not benefit from their misfortune by turning their feathers into high-priced fashion? All that is needed to put an "ethical stamp of approval" on this practice is to make the claim that the birds are traceable to farms that don't force feed or live pluck them. We can see how reductionism also plays into this story, that by eliminating certain unpopular and egregious forms of abuse the problem is solved. But it's not. It's still there. There may be some nicks on its finish, but the problem of exploiting and killing animals for our pleasure still lurks behind the façade.

NORMALITY

Perpetuating the idea that eating animals is normal is a critical factor in maintaining the legitimacy of the dominant culture's power over animals. In our consumerist age, the forces of popular culture are largely shaped by the market and those who have vested financial interests at stake. While portrayals of Old McDonald's Farm are ubiquitous, there is also a concerted effort to normalize industrial agriculture practices. Fair Oaks Farms in northwest Indiana is an unsettling example of an animal-agriculture brand that attempts to blur the distinction between tradition and modernity, describing itself as "an escape to the country with acres of great outdoor fun, food and learning where you can explore family farms and reconnect with nature, animals and our planet."[178] Author and activist Ashley Capps visited Fair Oaks Farms and shares her observations about her experience that day:

> On August 5, 2013, Fair Oaks Farms celebrated the Grand Opening of "Pig Adventure," a breeding facility where approximately 2,700 sows are confined and artificially inseminated to produce nearly 80,000 pigs for slaughter each year. Pig Adventure joins the Fair Oaks Dairy Adventure, a 36,000 dairy cow operation that has, since 2004, doubled as an "Agricultural Disney"; on daily tours, visitors

can watch calves being born, cows being milked on giant mechanized carousels, and cheese being made, among many other dairy-themed spectacles. And now, with help from major agribusiness backers (including the National Pork Board and Indiana Pork), visitors can also ooh and aah at the more than 200 piglets born daily, then head over to the farm's full restaurant for a Bacon and Swiss Grilled Cheese.

... [Y]ou could almost be fooled into thinking that Fair Oaks is some kind of Pig Appreciation and Protection Society: from the tour buses plastered with images of smiling, adorable pink piglets, to the exuberant animated pig who narrates Pig Adventure's website, to the reverential description of Pig Adventure's breeding and confinement operation as "The Miracle of Life Project." The founders of this facility say it's designed "to highlight the treatment and well being of pigs" and to demonstrate that "pork production is morally right, a noble profession and a service to humanity."[179]

On the other end of the farming spectrum is a place like Ernest's dairy farm off of Sir Francis Drake Boulevard in California's Point Reyes National Seashore. Anyone en route to the famous lighthouse could stumble upon his farm on the side of the road. Ernest is the son of a family that has owned this two-hundred-head dairy farm for many generations, producing all pasture-based, grass-fed, organic milk for customers like Trader Joe's. Ernest lives in the modest, old frame house right across the road from this dairy operation, the same house many generations of his family lived in. If you stop and visit the farm, he'll be happy to show you around and tell you all about the normal, day-to-day activities of a dairy farm like his. He'll show you the row of plastic hutches, each housing one newborn female calf who was immediately separated from her mother at birth. "The males are out of here right away," Ernest will explain. "We have someone who comes and picks them up. I have no idea where they go. The females here are all separated in their own hutch, so if one gets sick, she doesn't get all the others sick too." They look so terribly sad and alone.

The female calves will cautiously lick your hand through the fence and want to suckle. Others cower back into their plastic hutches, looking terrified and despondent. They are all just days or weeks old, in many ways like large puppies, only instead of bouncing around and wanting to play, their spirits are broken. You can see it in their eyes. Their mothers will be only forty or fifty feet away, but separated by the large milking parlor shed that blocks them from viewing one another. Ernest will proudly explain that he now does artificial insemination and breeds the cows himself. He'll explain how he keeps the cows only as long as they're producing more value in milk than the cost of feeding them. He recalls his grandfather telling him that the younger heifers produce better milk, so the younger, the better. "It's a really tough business," Ernest will confess. Lots of problems with the cows. Some can't get pregnant; others have complications with pregnancies, like stillborns, or they develop chronic diseases like mastitis, lameness, tumors, bovine leukemia, and distended udders that look like they are carrying milk but are just full of fat cells. None of these cows are economically viable, so they too, in their frail state, are picked up by the man he hires to take them where he has never been, where they are turned into hamburger. Ernest's matter-of-fact, businesslike demeanor will never hint at the fact that these animals in his care might be suffering. Having grown up in a family of dairy farmers for several generations, it is simply business as usual. It's a process of normalizing an entirely abnormal set of circumstances for the animals trapped in that production model.

Animal use is also normalized through public attractions, exhibits, and destinations sponsored or created by the animal exploitation industries in their effort to convey the perception of animal use as normal, wholesome, and transparent. Such is the case with Wagner Farm, a publicly funded, historic working dairy farm and museum just outside of Chicago in the affluent suburb of Glenview, with ties to local food industry titans like Kraft Foods and Oscar Mayer. Their annual bacon fest has featured bacon generously supplied by Oscar Mayer rather than from the piglets in their barn, allowing visitors to literally pet the piglets and sample the bacon all as part of the same experience. In short, Wagner Farm has evolved into a sophisticated "know-where-your-food-comes-from" farm education brand. The effect of visiting the farm leaves visitors feeling better about eating animals since they now have come face-to-face with their food, as if making the pilgrimage here somehow absolves them of the burden of the suffering we cause the other 99 percent of the animals we eat who are raised in standard industrial facilities. A place like Wagner Farm is also instrumental in providing a socialization testing ground for children, weaving together a number of powerful fictional devices—history, tradition, naturalism, and humane-washing—to create a compelling narrative around the theme of *doing farming right* or *farming with integrity*. Wagner Farm is managed by the Glenview Park District and funded largely with taxpayer dollars, which they have often proudly cited in response to criticism about poor treatment of their animals. Many of the animals now come to Wagner Farm from the local 4-H club, the Glenview Clovers, apparently the largest 4-H club in Illinois, with approximately 50 percent of the animal exhibits at the Lake County Fair. In response to numerous inquiries from visitors as to what happens to the baby animals in their exhibits, Wagner Farm explains that the 4-H animals there are intentionally removed from their facility at the end of the 4-H project season each summer and auctioned off at the Lake County Fair where they will be sold to the highest bidder for slaughter. Wagner Farm describes this as an important part of the "educational program" that the children and parents of the 4-H club fully understand and accept. But do they? In the next section, we'll take a closer look at this socialization process.

SOCIALIZATION

While most of us don't have any relationship with, let alone ever see, the animals who become the abstract edible objects we purchase in the store, it is revealing to look at those who do, who sometimes even claim to love the animals whose trust they will intentionally betray by sending them off to a violent and premature death in exchange for some financial reward. I use the term *socialization* in this context to refer to the set of fictional devices our culture uses to condition children and adults to accept the fate of the farmed animals they claim to care about as an inevitability. In this context, 4-H is of particular interest as a large-scale, institutionalized program of training and socializing young people that is deeply rooted in dominion. According to their website, "4-H is the nation's largest youth development organization, empowering six million young people throughout the United States."[180]

In a University of Colorado study, researchers Colter Ellis and Leslie Irvine explore the socialization process they found with children in 4-H programs. The authors describe their analysis as portraying "4-H as an apprenticeship in which children learn to do cognitive emotion work, use distancing mechanisms, and create a 'redemption' narrative to cope with contradictory ethical and emotional experiences."[181] While focused on children, the study also has larger implications: "An understanding of the means through which people learn to justify the treatment of the animals known as 'livestock' can shed light on the mechanisms involved in generic processes of inequality."

One young woman named Elizabeth shared with me in September 2013 her moving, intimate story about growing up in the 4-H program.

> I think a lot about what I did back in 4-H, how I basically treated those animals as commodities instead of sentient beings. While I wasn't unnecessarily cruel to them, I do remember getting some

first insights into their feelings. In those days of my youth, I chased one of the more human-friendly goats up on top of the climbing toy. She was too afraid to jump, so she turned around to face me as I came up on her and let out a resounding bleat. I could see in her eyes that she was pleading for me to stop. I felt like she spoke to my soul, so I did stop. I don't know why it didn't click with me then to respect all animals more, to not show them like they are objects, and to not send them off to slaughter. I also think about how I dragged all those terrified goats into the grooming stalls at the shows. I think about the sound of their choking and their attempts to escape. I remember their babies and the joy of those little ones as they entered the world. They didn't just walk around; they hopped and skipped with glee around the field. They would even bounce on top of their parents. And I remember my adorable, sweet cow Bobo. He was always happy to see us. Whenever he saw us outside he'd run up to the fence for kisses and licks. I can't believe what I sentenced him to. Whenever I go back to the fair grounds with my dad, it seems like such a grotesque place. Sure, the fair looks like a happy event, with children running around and many animals to see and people asking to come inside the pens to see the animals. But underlying this is a horrible prejudice toward and exploitation of sentient beings. Not too long ago I went to the fair with my dad and we came upon a live auction. My heart stopped, and I felt like I couldn't breathe. The image of leading Bobo around that loop of death was so clear in my mind. I didn't know what to do. I wanted to stop the auction, but I knew the

50 people there wouldn't let me do that. I felt awful — and still feel awful — for not having done something, anything. These fairs and shows and auctions are run by adults who believe they are doing a good thing in teaching their kids how to be farmers. But I think it's awful that we children are learning to see animals as property and possessions. Even though we are taught to take good care of our animal property, at the end of the day we willingly send innocent sentient beings to slaughter. When we show the animals, it's never for their own sake. We show their bodies, but never their inner worth as unique individuals with thoughts and feelings, with families and friends, and with a will to live that's just as strong as ours.

Across the spectrum of experience—from emotionally stirring personal anecdotes like Elizabeth's to academic research—socialization has proven immensely powerful over an influential youth. In an eye-opening research paper called "The Conceptual Separation of Food and Animals in Childhood," University of Bristol researchers Kate Stewart and Matthew Cole explore how we teach our children a separate morality for food animals that intercepts a child's natural and indiscriminate tendency to empathize with all animals. As the paper points out, when we explain to children for the first time where meat comes from, their first reaction is often revulsion. Parents confront this moral quandary by explaining to children why farmed animals have a different role in our lives than other animals and are therefore justified in receiving differential treatment. This familial conditioning, combined with other cultural and consumer advertising influences, "contribute to a food socialization process whereby children learn to conceptually distance the animals they eat from those with whom they have an emotional bond or for whom they feel ethically responsible."[182] Or, in other words, children learn which animals to love and which to eat, according to accepted social norms.

But this rigid moral framework doesn't make sense to all children. Recalling a terrifying childhood experience, one Facebook commentator wrote, "When I was very young, a pet pig who adopted me was taken to the slaughterhouse. It was humanely treated but it was stunned, decapitated and hung up by its legs and hacked apart lengthwise. This pig was my best friend, it was entrusted to me and I felt I had betrayed him. I was too young to realize that my parents would not do the same to me or my brother, so distrust, fears and nightmares were a regular occurrence for me." Stewart and Cole delve deep into how popular narratives define the role of farmed animals for children and how they define and differentiate them from the two other major categories of animals: wildlife and pets. In their examination of children's films like *The Lion King*, *Babe*, *Charlotte's Web*, *Chicken Run*, and *Bambi*, they carefully decode underlying moral constructs and messages that have a powerful impact on children via food-industry advertising and product offerings. In other words, these fictional messages flow cleverly from the movie screen to the Happy Meal box, which contains visuals and animal toys of those same film characters. Paradoxically, "farmed animals, invisible and unmentioned as they are in literature and film, lay invisible and unmentioned in the meal box in burger or nugget form."[183]

Stewart and Cole have identified at least five primary fictional devices that run through the narratives of most children's film, literature, and advertising, as follows:

1. Farmed animals are working animals, replaceable commodities, or just absent altogether, while carnivorous wild animals and pets are often endowed with highly developed characteristics that humanize them and therefore increase their perceived value.
2. Child characters regularly abandon empathy for animal characters with whom they have developed deep

bonds, as if this were a rite of passage to adulthood (a theme found in *My Friend Flicka* and *The Jungle Book*).

3. Animal characters are defined by their relative utility to humans. "Animals are saved," explains Stewart and Cole, "if they transcend their species-being, specifically if they attain human-like qualities."[184] Such transcendence occurs with the protagonists in *Babe*, *Chicken Run*, and *Happy Feet*, thus sparing them from their customary fate of being slaughtered.

4. Farmed animals are objects or elements of production devoid of individual characteristics. Evidence of this objectification can be seen in how advertisers and filmmakers refer to various types of meat as *pork* or *hamburger*, rather than by the name of the animal.

5. Humans are at the top of the food chain, whereby our consumption of the "lower" animals honors the "circle of life" (a theme central to *The Lion King*). In *The Lion King*, herbivorous animals have no names, no voices, no signs of intelligence, and no individual traits while the lions (being carnivores high up in the food chain) are highly developed and individualized characters. For Stewart and Cole, "*The Lion King* depicts a rigid and immutable hierarchical pattern of social relations, and meat-eating as not only natural, but a sacred duty to the 'circle of life.'"[185]

GREENWASHING

Like humane-washing, animal agriculture uses greenwashing by promoting the fiction that raising animals for food, even when compared to raising plants for food, can be done sustainably, a strategy we see them increasingly use to appeal to the growing ecological consciousness of consumers. The San Francisco–based website Civil Eats, *Mother Jones*, *Modern Farmer* and Whole Foods Market branding are all popular voices in the so-called sustainable locavore community. They don't simply advocate sustainable methods of animal agriculture more than conventional agribusiness, or what they like to call factory farming. They actually promote a variety of other sustainability-related fictions, ranging from the claim that farmed animals are necessary for fertilizing the soil to grow plant crops to claims that the environmental impact of tofu and soy-based meat alternatives are greater than their brand of sustainable animal agriculture. My goal here is not to address all of the fictions in this genre so much as it is to simply highlight a few common fictions that have become widely circulated and absorbed as fact by the general public.

One of these is the popular claim that plant agriculture needs animal manure to fertilize the soil and to create the yields necessary to grow enough food for large populations. In an article about the process by which soil becomes fertile, agriculture technology expert Steven Savage explains that "the animals didn't 'make' any of those nutrients. For instance the ~2% nitrogen in cow manure came from whatever they ate (grass, corn, soybeans) and those crops. . . ."[186] Savage, who is adamant about disassociating himself from the "vegan elite" (as he refers to them), nevertheless challenges the claim from organic animal farmers that manure produced from their animals is a more sustainable way to fertilize their crops over external inputs, pointing out that "they [organic farmers] are only ever going to be a small contributor to our overall fertilizer needs."[187] What he means is that organic, pasture-based animal agriculture will only ever serve a small, niche market because there isn't anywhere near enough arable land and water available to feed a global population this way. Today, most fertilizer is commercially produced not from animal manure but instead using the Bosch-Haber process that pulls nitrogen from the air.[188] According to the *Guardian*'s science editor, Robin McKie, "several billion people are alive today only because [Fritz] Haber found a way to turn atmospheric nitrogen into ammonia fertiliser. 'Bread from air,' ran the slogan that advertised his work at the time."[189]

Another poignant example of how greenwashing and humane-washing fictions comfortably coexist to prevent well-intentioned people from ever grasping the abysmal ecological impact of eating animals over plants can be found in an article on Civil Eats called "A More Humane Way to Breed Laying Hens" by author Brie Mazurek.[190] Mazurek interviews a farmer named Nigel Walker, owner of Eatwell Farm in Dixon, California, who explains his vision for a more sustainable, humane, pasture-based egg farm. For example, in response to his customers' frequent concerns over the killing of male chicks at the hatcheries that supply nearly all egg farms, from factory farms to backyard hen keepers, Walker plans to breed his own birds instead, and he's asking his supporters—consumers seeking the most humane, sustainable egg products—to fund his own hatchery project. Many of the fictions and claims made by both Mazurek and Walker in this article are representative of a much larger cultural trend, so let's take a look at some of these.

Mazurek: *"Many conscientious eaters go out of their way to purchase pasture-raised eggs laid by happy chickens."*
But a pasture isn't necessarily an idyllic habitat for chickens. Domestic chickens are most closely connected to their wild cousins the jungle fowl, who still inhabit tropical rain forests where they have evolved happily for thousands of years.[191] Their brains, behaviors, and natural instincts have been shaped by one of the most complex, diverse, and dynamic ecosystems on the planet. A largely treeless, open farm pasture is a stressful environment where chickens feel vulnerable and overexposed to predation. Reports on pasture-raised chickens show that they experience heightened cortisol levels (a stress hormone), indicating a fight or flight uneasiness.[192] In fact, it is the pasture farmers themselves who complain about the number of chickens they've lost to predators. In contrast, chickens in their natural rain forest habitat create their own social order that collectively—and very successfully—thwarts predators. Some studies have shown that chickens survive predator attacks 90 percent of

the time in their natural environment.[193] Forcing animals to live in an environment that is foreign to them and that places them in harm's way—and breaking up their natural social order so that we can exploit them for their eggs and flesh—is neither conscientious nor natural.

Walker: *"We are on a mission to put the old breeds of poultry back to work."* Mazurek: *"While such birds may produce fewer eggs and put on pounds more slowly than modern breeds, they tend to be more healthy, resilient, and productive in the long run."*

What Walker refers to as the *old breeds*, and what others sometimes refer to as *heritage breeds*, are still the product of centuries of selective breeding intended to manipulate them to lay an obscenely unnatural number of eggs. Consider that wild chickens, in stark contrast to these breeds, lay only a few clutches of eggs—ten to fifteen eggs per year.[194] Like all birds, they lay eggs only during breeding season and only for the purpose of reproduction.[195] As a result, these old breeds are still vulnerable to all the common disorders and diseases that afflict birds who have been more intensively bred, like leghorns. Sanctuaries that have collectively rescued thousands of these birds can attest to their frailty and susceptibility to disease.

Mazurek: *"As the flock grows, the birds must be carefully tracked. Each time a hen goes to lay an egg, a door closes behind her (in what is called a trap nest) so that the bird and her egg can be recorded by Eatwell staff. The best of the best will be selected for hatching."*

There is essentially no difference in the intent and practice of breeding chickens for specific traits in Walker's method described by Mazurek, and the selective breeding methods used by industrial hatcheries that farmers like Walker already claim to oppose. Both rely on dominating and exploiting the female reproductive system, weeding out "inferior" animals in favor of those with "superior" traits, with the goal of increasing productivity and profit. The end goal is still one of more efficient exploitation. If we were to apply this same mentality and methodology to our treatment of certain human groups, we would be looking at something like the eugenics programs of Nazi scientists and ideologues who promoted a vision of an "optimal" Aryan race. If it's immoral to dominate and manipulate human animals in such a manner, then how can it be moral to control and modify nonhuman animals in this way, particularly when the latter have no way of consenting?

Mazurek: *"The males will be raised to maturity and processed for meat, providing additional income for the farm."*
How does Walker define *maturity*? What does that mean for a bird with a natural lifespan of eight to twelve years? How many weeks is he allowed to live past the mere six weeks of life of a typical broiler chicken on an industrial farm? A few more weeks, perhaps? If so, he is still in his infancy. Walker pretends he's doing the male chicks a favor by letting them mature into slightly older infants before he sends them to slaughter for additional revenue for his farm.

Walker: *"Chickens play an invaluable role in the farm's ecosystem, having eliminated the need for compost and external fertilizers."*
Since when is a farm a natural ecosystem? And why would you want to eliminate compost, nature's own free fertilizer, and replace it with excrement from domestic invasive species? According to sustainability expert Will Anderson, "at Eatwell Farm, chickens may be indispensable to the egg and chicken meat business, but not to an ecosystem. In the far more limited sense, chickens do cycle nutrients back to the soil, but those nutrients required the artificial addition of more energy and water intensive inputs in the form of 30 tons of organic wheat grown specifically to feed the chickens. Eatwell's 'agro-ecosystem' does not increase biomass for the ecosystem, but removes much of it when sold as food and the chickens are taken to slaughter."[196]
Walker: *"The real core issue here is getting animals back on farms and out of these confinement operations. . . . Yes, we want their eggs, and the*

meat is great, too, but the reason we have our chickens is that they eat the pasture and fertilize the ground. All our organic vegetables are grown with fertility from cover crops and chickens."

Again, a response from Will Anderson: "Veganic agriculture provides the compost for crops minus the waste of wheat [used for chicken feed] and loss of chicken and dairy lives while using less energy, land, and water. Like others who celebrate animal agriculture, Nigel Walker seems not to ask what could be better. As a result, they overlook the fact that these practices are not sustainable given the extent of global ecosystem destruction, and, more obviously, are not needed as food."[197]

Walker: *"We're trying to find a bird that can live outside, where it can express all of its chickenness."*

Where can chickens actually express "all of their chickenness?" Well, we can turn to sanctuaries that have rescued these birds from the farming industry and that value them, not as units of production but for their intrinsic value as autonomous individuals who have names and unique personalities. And as we have seen in chapter 2, there is a wealth of scientific study revealing what chickens are really like in their natural habitat.

Chapter 7:

Leveraging Truth to Fight Fictions

With a deeper awareness of the fictions so far discussed in this book and an interest in sharing what we learn, what happens when we confront the fictional world of eating animals? This chapter first looks at the backlash we can expect and tips for overcoming it. Then we examine some key insights that have been absent from or unrecognized by mainstream animal advocacy that animal advocates can use to strengthen their work

SHOOTING THE MESSENGER

"While vegans have a right to express their opinion — and we respect that right — they should not force their lifestyle on others,"[198] said David Warner of the National Pork Council in response to an Associated Press story in which he was asked about his thoughts on animal activists. When we expose and challenge animal agriculture's fictions, their spokespeople go on the defensive and work hard to leverage the power they have over popular culture. Sometimes this translates into attacking animal advocates for "pushing their agenda," "forcing their ideas down our throat," or "spreading propaganda." So why don't other social justice advocates face the same accusations? It is telling that human rights activists who campaign against violent and exploitative practices, such as sweatshop labor or sex trafficking, are rarely, if ever, criticized for pushing their beliefs on others. On the contrary, these activists are lauded for their passion and commitment to justice and for exposing injustices. So why is it that when we advocate against the same kind of violent and exploitative practices perpetrated against other animals, we are suddenly "forcing ideas down their throats?" With billions of lives at stake and an unprecedented scale of institutionalized violence against innocent victims being waged largely in silence and out of sight, is the appropriate response to hand out recipes for vegan chocolate mousse? How would we react, or expect others to react, if the victims were humans instead? Why do we shoot the messenger, attack the whistleblower, and thereby ignore or trivialize the victims?

It's clear that such responses are based in speciesism, but believing that human suffering and human lives are worth more than the suffering and lives of other animals does not negate all moral consideration for them. It does not justify systematically exploiting, killing, and eating them. Characterizing animal advocates as the problem is part of a concerted effort to invalidate the animal liberation movement and reinforce social and cultural norms. It's a reaction social psychologist Melanie Joy calls secondary carnistic defenses.[199] As Joy explains, "secondary defenses are a part of a backlash against veganism; a backlash is a reaction of the dominant culture when its power is threatened."[200]

When faced with this kind of reaction, animal advocates would do well to shift the focus of attention back on where it belongs: the victims. The undeniable truth is that these critics who claim that we are forcing our views on them are already paying someone to literally force-feed animals, impregnate females by force, separate babies from mothers by force, force them to live in confinement and/or their own filth, mutilate their beaks, hooves, genitalia, tails, toes, ears, and teeth by force, transport them to slaughter by force, and violently take their lives by force. People who buy animal products inadvertently pay for abuse of power and influence on many levels they don't see or choose not to see, each and every time they buy an animal product. But no one can force you to accept an idea.

According to professor and philosopher Mylan Engel, most people already believe that animals should not be made to suffer for no good reason and that we should minimize the harm we do to others, even in cases where inflicting harm is necessary. As a logical consequence of this belief, Engel's central message is "Your beliefs and values already commit you to the immorality of eating meat."[201] In other words, we already accept that we should avoid harming animals unnecessarily and especially in cases where someone derives pleasure from that harm. Since eating animals represents 99.7 percent of the animals needlessly harmed by humans,[202] we cannot, in good faith, selectively exclude farmed animals from this harm reduction/avoidance principle.

Ultimately, the real source of power and influence is staring us in the face: just follow the money. Those who have the most financial interest in protecting an unethical practice, like exploiting and killing innocent animals or exploiting workers in sweatshop factories, must invest great effort and resources in concealing the ugly truth of their enterprise. As mentioned in chapter 1, Cargill alone spent $1.792 billion just on promoting animal products to consumers in the course of 2012.[203] Propaganda is a tool used by those in a position of power to influence and deceive the public by masking a violent reality with feel-good fictions. It is therefore foolhardy to compare a small vocal minority, such as animal advocates or vegans, with the industries that spend billions of dollars in marketing annually to create a propaganda machine powerful enough to brainwash 98 percent of consumers, including those with higher-education degrees who otherwise think critically on other important social issues.

First-World Critiques

Dismissal and marginalization are popular critiques of animal advocacy. At one of my recent presentations, someone raised the point during the Q & A that a concern for animals is a first-world concern. Aside from the obvious prejudice in the use of terms such as *first world* and *third world*, for our purposes, let's just focus here on its implication that advocating for animals is a frivolous issue compared with much bigger global problems, and one that only affluent people have the luxury to think about. Notice how we hear this criticism only in reaction to farmed-animal advocates who represent the 99 percent of animals exploited by humans, and rarely, if ever, for wildlife or companion-animal protection. The fact is that many non-first-world countries have sought protections for animals far beyond our first-world standards, proving that you don't need to be affluent to care about and defend animals.

In the case of Cecil the lion, the Zimbabwe government cared enough about the issue to seek the extradition of his perpetrator so that they may try him in a high court (even though the effort was eventually dropped). The efforts to save feral dogs from brutal killing in Romania and Russia are not criticized as a first-world concern. What's really "first world" is our fetish for buying designer, purebred dogs while millions of other dogs languish on death row in shelters. What's really "first world" is a multi-million-dollar doggie day care and products industry that caters to our obsession with showering our pets with toys and professional beauty treatments, while we ignore the plight of billions of other animals we pay to be brutalized and killed for our daily food choices.

This first-world critique appears to be consistent with condemning white or Western privilege and the disparity between the world's haves and have nots while being rooted in human prejudice and privilege itself—prejudice based on species membership. The fact is that humans are animals too, and we aren't the only animals who suffer or who have lives that matter to us. The first-world critique is often coupled with the false dilemma that human interests compete with other animals, when in fact the 99 percent of animals we harm are those we eat for reasons of pleasure, not out of necessity or competition to protect important human interests. In short, they don't need us to tear ourselves away from solving our own human problems to help them. No, they just need us to leave them alone and stop buying them, which will result in them no longer being bred in the first place. Problem solved for the 99 percent.

Finally, many other social justice issues have their roots in the first world too, like justice for sweatshop laborers, battered women, and date rape victims; gay rights and gay marriage; hate crime; bullying; and equal pay for women. But notice how advocates for these causes are never criticized as "first world." On the contrary, they are often lauded for their brave work to expose and fight against these injustices. If anything deserves to be critiqued as a first-world issue, it is ironically the same one these critics defend:

the Western animal-based diet, which has been relentlessly marketed beyond the first world by those who profit from spreading chronic disease, exacerbating world hunger, creating political instability, wreaking ecological degradation and, of course, inflicting a massive scale of animal suffering around the globe. What's truly "first world" is animal agriculture's aggressive marketing of animal products in areas of the world that have traditionally eaten animal products only marginally. And the only thing the so-called progressives can think of criticizing is farmed-animal advocates, while ignoring the actual abusers.

INSIGHTS FOR ANIMAL ADVOCATES

Once we become aware of how popular culture manipulates our beliefs and the food choices that stem from them, many of us want to know how all of this can inform animal advocacy. While this book is not intended as a guide for animal advocates, the implications here are nonetheless compelling and relevant. This section provides a snapshot of the prevailing trends in animal advocacy and compares them against *truth-centeredness*, a strategy I will explain more fully later on that emerges organically from the fiction-fact dynamic between the fictional world of animal agriculture set against the reality of the animal's experience. The most important takeaway from this book is that ideas matter. Beliefs matter.

In evaluating all of the fictional examples presented in this book, we find one important common thread connecting them: they all appeal to our deeply held beliefs and values about farmed animals, our role as humans in the world, and eating as a daily social and cultural ritual. And this strategic appeal to our beliefs and values is spectacularly successful, considering the fact that most of us have assimilated them into our consciousness and spout them back out to others, as if they were fact, and with little or no critical evaluation. The food industry accomplishes this by studying popular trends, beliefs, and values about food and animals and crafting them into compelling fictional narratives. In other words, we tell them what we want to believe, see, and hear, and they reflect that reality back to us through sophisticated branding campaigns that seduce us into not just buying their products or services but actually *believing* in their brands. In leadership expert Simon Sinek's acclaimed TED Talk "How Great Leaders Inspire Action," he says repeatedly, "People don't buy *what* you do; they buy *why* you do it."[204] For Sinek, the *why* is that passion, belief, or idea that drives us. Successful brands develop brand loyalists because of their focus on the *why*, a technique they've borrowed from leaders of social movements. Sinek shows us how brands like Apple as well as the Wright Brothers and Martin Luther King Jr. all derived their incredible influence by focusing on their *why*.

The second most important takeaway is that animal advocates need to become skilled at successfully challenging and disempowering this fictional world in order to achieve the meaningful and lasting change we long for. From my twenty years of working as a marketing communications/branding professional, I've acquired a behind-the-scenes perspective on how food and other brands are built on fictions like those identified earlier in this book. In general, corporate branding offers us some valuable lessons that I believe we can use to our advantage, yet it is important to recognize that brand building is based on a fundamental deception or subversion of reality, both in principle and in practice, that, when applied to animal advocacy, could sabotage our credibility and integrity. Soon after I entered the world of animal advocacy, I was struck by how eagerly nonprofits and certain advocacy organizations embraced this corporate model of communications and branding, as if it were the gold standard for our own success or failure, without much concern over how its fundamental motivations might conflict with the goals of a social movement like ours. While our primary objective is to break through society's collective silence, denial, and defensiveness about animal exploitation and build a consensus around animal liberation, corporate branding is driven by market forces that are often disturbingly in conflict with our objective and the objectives of other social justice causes. In the case of animal-product branding, there is a concerted effort to invert the truth, to present suffering as contentment, to mask an inherently violent and exploitative practice with a happy animal fantasy.

The Behaviorist Model

One of the more troubling realities we face is a persistently low vegan population coupled with an allegedly high rate of vegan recidivism, according to some recent research.[205] Set against these statistics is an emerging approach to animal advocacy that emphasizes effectiveness as its overarching virtue, achieved through an ongoing analysis and refinement of our tactics, strategies, and approaches. From this point on, we will refer to the adherents of this approach as the behaviorists. The behaviorists insist that effective advocacy is based on studies or research they design about how consumers react to various advocacy approaches, and an evaluation of charities to create a new breed of "smart" donors. And yet even they will occasionally admit that measuring effectiveness becomes an incredibly complex challenge, which begs the question: Exactly how do they define *effective*? What we come to learn is that *effective* is a code word for a more business-minded pragmatism, rather than any comprehensive analysis of all of the major forms of activism employed effectively by other social movements.

Having a clear bottom line, they claim, is also key to effectiveness, such as the very popular bottom line "Saving the greatest number of animals" (yet another immensely difficult metric to quantify, let alone attribute to a specific advocacy approach). Predictably, their own studies frequently conclude that their own approaches are more effective than others studied. Such a methodology has paid off handsomely for the food industry, which has invested a great deal in market research, focus groups, surveys, direct mail, e-mail, and social media engagement, all in an effort to better understand their target market and determine how best to sell their products. And even nonprofits stand much to gain from the valuable insights that result from the same analysis in an effort to grow donor support. In fact, earlier in the book we looked at specific cases of how the same fictional devices from animal agriculture have been appropriated by certain nonprofits. At the same time, important questions should be raised about this approach, such as "What exactly do we as animal advocates, as part of a movement for animal liberation, expect to gain from asking those who willingly support an injustice what approach or what information will be most effective in getting their attention?," "How can we expect them to provide thoughtful insights into an injustice that thrives on their very denial and silence?," and finally, "Can such a corporate model for increasing consumer brand loyalty and selling more products really so seamlessly apply to the advancement of a social justice movement?"

Ironically, the behaviorists characteristically overlook the essential lesson from corporate branding at the core of this book—that appealing to beliefs and values is the most powerful way brands influence popular culture and our food choices—and focus instead on how they can shift consumer dietary behavior without any awkward or messy confrontation with the beliefs behind it. This commonly manifests itself in purely diet-focused, "baby-step" branding campaigns, like Meatless Mondays and Vegan Before 6. In essence, behaviorism focuses on what Simon Sinek refers to as the *how* rather than the *why*: the key reason, he says, leaders fail.[206] But without grasping the *why* of veganism, new vegan recruits have no compelling reasons for a long-term commitment, which may account for the reportedly high rates of vegan recidivism.[207] Behaviorists still insist that it doesn't matter *why* someone gets there, as long as they *get there*. But they're not staying there, and why should we expect anything different when we characterize veganism as just another personal dietary choice? Meanwhile, our animal-eating culture continues to pummel these defectors with powerful fictions against which such a behaviorist approach is powerless.

Another popular idea among behaviorists is the framing of advocacy today as a spectrum between effectiveness and moral or philosophical purity. This is often expressed in statements like "Do you want results or do you want to be right?" In such a false dilemma, theory is made useless and divorced from action. Ideas and principles are just "personal issues" that get in the way of results. In his book *Change of Heart*, Nick Cooney presents a conflict between our desire for self-expression or ego fulfillment and our goal of effective advocacy for animals. But the very desire to be effective itself is just as much driven by self-expression or ego as any other pursuit. All social justice advocacy qualifies as self-expression. Great leaders and visionaries of social movements express the intellectual and moral leadership that rally activists to the cause and motivate them to carry out their work. Yet rather than seeking inspiration from these change leaders and visionaries, behaviorists look to corporate models of efficiency. Not surprisingly, their idea of effectiveness based on a dampening of self-expression leads to a shallow conformism that stifles the creativity, free thinking, brainstorming, and individual expression needed to develop the most effective ideas and leaders. In this environment, an appreciation for the power of the beliefs and ideologies behind eating animals is often stigmatized and criticized as selfish, egotistical, self-indulgent, wishful thinking, or ineffective.

Behaviorists envision themselves guiding society, incrementally, to a plant-based diet, relying on the foot-in-the-door technique—yet another tactic borrowed from corporate sales and marketing, which they rather erroneously apply to animal advocacy. But as much as animal advocates like Cooney insist that the FITD technique is so effective on experimental applications in animal advocacy,[208] the sentiment in the social psychology community, even for traditional applications of FITD, remains skeptical at best. In fact, researchers from Santa Clara University found that "research on the foot-in-the-door technique is far from consistent or easy to interpret. The literature is filled with failures to replicate and occasional reversals of effect."[209] Yet another study published in the *Journal of Consumer Research* states that "the findings from scientific studies on the foot-in-the-door technique have been mixed. Although some studies have found that the foot-in-the-door technique can increase donations, other studies found no statistically significant effect for the foot-in-the-door technique on donations."[210]

Then there's the opposite technique, what is known in social psychology as the door-in-the-face technique, in which the persuader attempts to convince the respondent to comply by making a large request that the respondent will most likely turn down, followed by smaller requests that the respondent will be more likely to accept. An example of how this might apply to animal advocacy would be, say, to call for the replacement, rather than the reduction, of animal products in our diets. One might ask how FITD and DITF techniques compare in terms of overall effectiveness, yet on this point Cooney and other fans of FITD are conspicuously silent. One leading social psychologist, James Dillard, concluded that the results of a comparative analysis of the effectiveness of FITD and DITF techniques did not show one more effective over the other.[211] Moreover, even if one aspired to this traditional "sales and marketing" path to animal advocacy, as do the large animal-advocacy organizations, the behaviorist reliance on FITD appears to be based on cherry-picking research to fit their desired approach and then disseminating it as "evidence-based" and "rigorously scientific."

Even if the research were more in favor of it, the FITD technique, when applied to something like animal advocacy, seems overly paternalistic, if not manipulative, as if expressing the sentiment "we know what's best for you" or "you can't handle the whole truth or see the big picture, so I'll feed it to you in stages." One wonders if, in their evaluation of effectiveness, the behaviorists considered how this technique has the potential to backfire when subjects become aware that this technique has been used on them. The FITD technique is also the basis for negotiations with the animal exploitation industries—and the legislators involved—to implement stages of animal welfare reform, all of which is justified as a move to alleviate, at the very least, the worst forms of animal abuse.

Perhaps the behaviorist fixation on diet can be partially explained by their belief that self-gratification overwhelms our moral consideration for other animals, or ethical matters in general, but this notion that people don't care contradicts so many studies reaffirming our high level of concern for animal suffering.[212] Or perhaps behaviorists set the bar so low because any marginal step forward can be framed as a win, and a series of small wins maintains morale by promising the larger, desired win at some time in the future. It's as if they've thrown in the towel, cynical about any real shift away from our intensely consumerist, narcissistic culture, as if it were static, unchangeable, and therefore undefeatable, rather than a mere blink in the span of human history. Perhaps they've given up on the prospect for radical social change, a resignation that may also result from an indifference to the great ideas from which we can gain inspiration, just as advocates of other social movements have. In any case, we can get a better understanding of their modus operandi by taking a closer look at two prominent behaviorist campaigns, effective altruism and reducetarianism.

Effective Altruism: An Exercise in Reductionism

According to pioneering philosopher Peter Singer, effective altruism is a social movement that seeks to help people make informed donations to the most effective charities. Sounds like a great idea, and straightforward enough—at least on the surface. But when we reflect on this idea a bit more, we might ask what exactly makes a charity effective? This is where things get foggy.

Let's just say, for the sake of comparison, charity A develops a catchy claim that it can save one farmed animal for every dollar you donate. Charity B, in contrast, has no easily quantifiable way to measure the impact of your donation, but nonetheless releases a viral documentary about farmed animals on a shoestring budget. Of course, charity B can measure some aspects of its impact, like how many views, downloads, likes, shares, or comments its web-based video generated, but this would represent, at best, only part of its overall impact. Charity B can't realistically translate these metrics into something as definitive as the number of animal lives saved by its documentary. Yet viewers consistently praise the film as "life-changing," claiming they could never *unlearn* what they learned from that film, never go back to supporting animal exploitation by eating or wearing animals again. Some even claim it has emboldened them into becoming activists. The film appears at several leading film festivals and receives much press coverage and reviews. On the other hand, with charity A, their donors were sold on the claim that their gift saved a certain number of animal lives, but they don't necessarily feel that charity A had a life-altering impact on them. Consequently, few of them feel compelled to share what they've learned. Regardless, charity A is rated as a "top charity" by the effective altruist rating model while charity B is not even rated, because they offer the evaluator no clear, quantifiable metric by which to measure their effectiveness. And, as a result, charity A brings in twenty times more donor dollars than charity B. The point of this hypothetical scenario is that, given the impossibility of realistically measuring all the factors that constitute overall impact of an individual advocate or organization, making the claim that charity A is more effective than charity B based on one specific metric—one farmed animal saved for every dollar donated—is invalid. The only case in which we could claim that charity A is more effective than charity B would be if we could take into account their aggregate impact on changing society's attitudes and eating behavior.

This is not to say that donors should not make well-researched and informed decisions about where they donate or that we should not evaluate charities, but rather that we should be honest about the immense complexity of measuring effectiveness or impact before we start handing out awards and prizes for the "most effective" or "best" individuals or organizations based on what amounts to a crude evaluation that hinges on just one limited impact to the exclusion of all other factors that contribute to overall effectiveness. In reality, the social sciences don't yet offer us the definitive results we would like for determining what is most effective for social justice advocacy. And it is unrealistic to think that such a corporate-based model for measuring effectiveness, one that was designed specifically to measure products and services, can sufficiently inform advocates and donors about how best to carry out a social justice movement. Such a model misses the forest for the trees, ignoring the causes of social injustices while stressing the need for tangible results. In some ways, it recalls the dead-end logic of conventional Western medicine, so absorbed in the treatment of symptoms that it never determines the illness or what causes it.

Reducetarianism: Lowering the Bar

One exceptionally popular form of behaviorism is reducetarianism, which is based on the premise that not everyone is willing or *able* to replace meat in their diets, and since the perception of vegans and vegetarians is largely negative anyway, the best solution is to advocate meat reduction. A key proponent of this movement is Brian Kateman, president of the Reducetarian Foundation, who lays out his strategy in a TED Talk called "Ending the Battle between Vegans, Vegetarians, and Everyone Else."[213] Another popular effort is from the Humane League Labs, which conducts "direct testing to improve vegan advocacy efforts" and "to figure out which images, messages, and approaches inspire the most diet change and spare the greatest number of farm animals."[214] HLL describes its approach as "rigorously applying the scientific method" to a movement which "has relied mainly on assumptions and anecdotes to guide their work."[215] On the surface, their mission sounds motivated by objective, unbiased inquiry, yet a closer look at their studies and affiliations with other advocates and organizations reveals that HLL's study designs, interpretation of data, and conclusions are all too often subjectively in favor of their own behaviorist brand of advocacy. Contrary to HLL's assertion, the animal movement, rather than guided by mere "anecdotes" and "assumptions," has an incredibly rich lexicon of research, theory, strategy, and vision to build upon, dating back to ancient times. It also has a rich body of evidence, lessons, and insights to gain from past and present social justice movements.

Some Practical Considerations

Since reducetarianism prides itself on being more pragmatic, let's look at a few pragmatic issues related to the reducetarian position and then look more closely at some issue related to psychology, strategy, and results. First, consider reducetarianism's audience, which is overwhelmingly Americans and Europeans, who shop in stores with a wide variety of products, including plant-based alternatives to flesh, dairy, and eggs, which have enjoyed tremendous growth in recent years and are projected to grow significantly in the years to come.[216] Under such circumstances, and for purely practical reasons, why would we advocate for reduction when replacing animal products with plant-based alternatives means simply reaching for a different place on the store shelf—when, in fact, replacement could actually be far easier than reduction? Reaching for a different place on the store shelf does not require an act of moral purity, hardship, or even inconvenience, as the reducetarian approach suggests; nor are plant-based alternatives difficult to find for the vast majority of us. It is not as if they can't provide us with satisfaction in both taste and texture, as well as provide equal or better nutrition and easily substitute in our favorite recipes. In fact, some of them are eerily indistinguishable from animal flesh and secretions. But even if reducing could be proven to be more effective than replacement, most people do a poor job of tracking the amount of any particular food group they consume. Many people may tell you that they already eat very little meat, but in reality their overall intake of animal products is present in some form in just about every meal.[217]

Reducetarians claim that the logic behind advocating meat reduction is partly to "end the battle" (as in the title of Kateman's

TED Talk), to remove the barriers between animal eaters and vegans or to make the perception of eating less animals friendlier and more inclusive, which, they believe, will encourage more people to take that path. But could setting the bar lower, or aiming for the lowest common denominator, really be more effective in helping animals over, say, a clear, concise, and targeted message of going plant-based? Successful corporate brands consistently use the latter strategy while lesser brands often fail by relying on a "shotgun approach," trying to be the brand that pleases every audience. There is something deeply flawed and patronizing in the notion that advocates set the bar for others, however low or high. Isn't this the real wishful thinking—believing that people will do exactly as we say? Isn't it wiser to assume that people will set the bar where they choose, usually lower than we would ask them to anyway? If one believes this to be true, then diluting our message will lead to a less effective impact on others.

From a practical standpoint, what better time than the present to advocate a vegan rather than a reducetarian message? We live in an age in which eating a plant-based diet is accessible to most of us, an age in which our planet demands swift and significant changes in our dietary behavior, and an age in which political and economic instability is intensifying over food and water shortages and disparities between rich and poor. After exploiting animals for some ten thousand years now, when, if not now, is the *right* time to advocate veganism?

Some Perceptual Considerations
Reducetarianism creates more psychological obstacles for people to get from point A to point B by reinforcing the false notion that adopting a plant-based diet is *so hard,* or *so extreme,* or can only be accomplished in stages. In reality, replacement is often as simple as reaching for one product over another on the store shelf. For that reason, animal advocates do not need to become the enablers for animal eaters to effectively engage them. The last thing animal eaters need is our help in fabricating excuses to avoid making the

switch, and the last thing animal advocates need to do is enable animal eaters to avoid the issue of animal victimization or indulge animal eaters in their exaggerated "hardship" of making some simple and straightforward dietary replacements. Transitioning to a plant-based diet is not a change that most of us will look back on as a great trial. The hard part is changing not one's diet but the beliefs that inform the diet.

Another perceptual challenge that we must overcome, says reducetarianism, is the negative perception of vegans and vegetarians as judgmental, pushy, and moralistic. But if we've learned anything from other social causes, then surely we can appreciate the fact that all advocates of change are criticized and attacked for having a different vision of justice for an oppressed group that society doesn't yet regard as worthy of consideration. In other words, it's par for the course. What Kateman seems to mean by "ending the battle between vegans, vegetarians, and everyone else" is to ignore the connection between beliefs and actions so as to present their platform as a safe and morally neutral space for everyone. A similar sentiment comes across in a Human League Labs study, where researchers compared different messaging and concluded that "the data from the current study suggest that the combination message of 'cut out or cut back on' meat and other animal products may be more effective than encouraging 'vegetarian' or 'vegan' eating for getting people to reduce animal product consumption."[218] Is it any surprise that asking people to do less of something they want to do will be perceived as more desirable than asking them to eliminate or replace that something, especially when the compelling reasons to make a change aren't part of the discourse? If we ask the hunting establishment to only hunt on Mondays and Tuesdays, and we don't make any moral judgments about blowing the heads off of deer, would they not be more likely to consider such a proposal over one that would place an outright ban on hunting? Of course people who eat animals and want to continue doing so will perceive "cutting back on meat" as more desirable than going vegan.

Instead of using trickery or cleverly framed messaging, we could instead focus on the compelling ethical reasons for and benefits of eating a plant-based diet, considering how compelling those reasons are. But more importantly, the problem with the reducetarian assertion that vegans have been stigmatized is that language itself is not static or fixed but continually evolving in meaning and context. As we've already seen through the many examples in this book, corporate branding is a testament to how language and message can be strategically used to alter the perception of even the most violent and oppressive realities into "happy" and "humane" ones. Similarly, through repetition and positive association, animal advocacy and some plant-based food brands are creating authentic perceptions of everyday vegans whom others aspire to be like. And as the word *vegan* continues to proliferate, it will inevitably enjoy more mainstream acceptance.

More Key Words That Equivocate

On the subject of reducetarian language, we should take a closer look at two key words: *meat* and *diet*. In the Humane League Labs study of messaging discussed earlier and in HLL's mission statement itself, notice that the specific focus is on "what inspires the most diet change."[219] As a result of this, the HLL researchers draw conclusions about the effectiveness of vegan messaging as if veganism were nothing more than a diet. The study claims to evaluate what words might be most effective in terms of influencing people to make a dietary change, not necessarily about veganism as a position against exploitation, as it has been customarily defined. In author Casey Taft's critique of this study, "a major overarching problem with this research is that veganism is not properly represented. A vegan messaging approach would not only focus on 'factory farming' but would discuss the ethics of using animals in all ways. It would also not focus on health. So again, if the authors are going to make any inferences about vegan messaging and its effectiveness, then truly vegan messaging should be employed."[220]

The word *diet* suggests a regimen that someone will take for a fixed period of time, perhaps one of many that someone will try for a while, go on and off of, and probably not take seriously. And a diet is something we do directly to benefit ourselves, while veganism is something we adopt as a way of life that directly benefits others and the planet. In other words, choosing plant foods is the logical manifestation of our objection to gratuitous animal suffering. HLL's focus on diet here is symptomatic of the larger problem of evaluating behavior as if it were detached from beliefs. Yet, as this book emphasizes, if our beliefs about eating animals don't change, we have no compelling reason to stick with a diet that may benefit animals and the planet. Perhaps this accounts for the high levels of vegan recidivism. Just like we can't cure a disease by masking the symptoms, we also can't create a better world for animals as long as *diet* remains the buzzword. We must successfully challenge and disempower the belief system upon which animal exploitation is built and food choices are made.

In chapter 3 we considered several popular cultural euphemisms, including our culture's pervasive naming of other animals as *meat*. As author Carol Adams points out, the word *meat* has a strategic power that renders a someone into a no one. "Meat, after all, has no power. It is the opposite of power; it is what happens to someone who has no power," she writes.[221] However, in certain contexts, the word *meat* makes sense and is perhaps unavoidable. For example, when referring to the meat industry, the word *meat* is qualified and understood as the industry that turns animals into abstract meat products. However, for animal advocates, using the word *meat*, without context, is disturbingly dissonant and could mislead others into thinking that we somehow sanction animal exploitation. Here we find ourselves inadvertently using the commodification fiction we find in flesh branding, which conflicts with our message of animals as "someone, not something." In its study of what messages are most effective at changing diet, HLL failed to consider how words like *meat* could undermine not just effectiveness but credibility and clarity. In other words, it fails to assess the unintended, adverse reactions to messaging that employs industry terms like *meat*. It also fails to consider the extent to which we, as messengers, and our audience care about the moral inconsistency involved in asking people to just reduce meat consumption, implying that it's okay to pay farms to use and kill animals some of the time, if not all of the time. Our critics are continually looking for our flaws and inconsistencies, pointing to products we use containing animal by-products like computers and to behavior like driving that harms animals. The message of meat reduction gives them more fodder to work with. In the end, reducetarianism promises better results—the saving of more animal lives—by paradoxically borrowing some of the same trickery and tactics used by corporate brands that condition us to eat animals.

The Perfection Myth

One of the most damaging misconceptions of veganism, and one that presents an immense obstacle for its more widespread adoption, is the characterization of veganism as a state of moral perfection or purity. We've looked closely at how popular culture fabricates the vegan perfection fiction in previous chapters. The fact that being vegan is often stigmatized as being "purist" or "perfectionist" from the perspective of popular culture is unsurprising, but when behaviorists in the animal movement identify vegan advocacy as perfection or purity, not only does this sabotage our credibility as a whole, it strengthens the fictions that condition people to continue eating animals. Veganism is far from perfection. Being vegan is a huge step in the right direction with very little effort proportionate to its immensely positive impact, but it's actually not the most we can do for animals and the planet. It is the least we can do. The very least we can do is spare animals the most gratuitous and needless forms of suffering through our daily food and lifestyle choices. There is much more that we can and must do for animals (including the human ones) and our planet beyond being vegan.

Replacing eggs, dairy, and animal flesh in our diet (and choosing non-animal-based personal care and apparel) is neither the pursuit of, nor the attainment of, perfection. Again, for many of us, it is simply a matter of reaching for a different product on the store shelf. *Perfection* could perhaps be defined as a state in which we have zero impact on animals and the planet, but that is currently not a possibility, and therefore it is not part of a realistic vegan position. By going vegan, we will not become perfect or even cruelty-free. We will, however, just by making some simple dietary and lifestyle changes, have reduced an enormous amount of suffering to innocent beings who have done nothing to us.

The fact that veganism remains a lifestyle practiced by a precious 1–2 percent of our population seems to contribute to its false characterization as perfection or purity. We can see from other social movements how the mob mentality has attacked small, vocal minorities advocating social justice with the same accusations in an attempt to smear them as extremists, yet those cases are equally unwarranted. Just because an idea is not popular does not make it pure or perfect or any less valid. As a consequence of our small population, we tend to exaggerate the hardship of going vegan. Yet, relative to the hardships that life can throw at us, going vegan is a walk in the park. Losing a loved one, going through a divorce, being fired from a job, or suffering a major personal injury or illness are difficult and challenging life experiences. On the contrary, eating according to your values and enjoying the food as well is cause for celebration. As author and activist Ashley Capps writes, "To be presented with the option to cause drastically less harm and suffering in the world: isn't this a gift? Shouldn't the opportunity to refrain from exploiting and killing others be embraced with swiftness and gratitude, rather than greeted with excuses for continuing to inflict gratuitous violence on others?"[222]

ADVOCACY AS COMMODITY?

In *The Postmodern Prince*, social change and political scholar John Sanbonmatsu presents a startling analysis of what he calls the commodification of knowledge, describing a higher-education system that has developed into a kind of think tank or research arm for corporate interests.[223] In the end, the market dictates what knowledge, what ideas get published and promoted. The market favors not the best ideas or even those that would create a better, more just world, but rather those that have the potential to be the most popular. The same circumstances apply to the state universities operating as nonprofits yet competing with private universities for students and research grants. The idea that this phenomenon should cross over into nonprofit culture, and animal advocacy specifically, isn't so surprising. In fact, many leading nonprofits already measure both advocacy and advocates on the basis of how commodities perform and collaborate with powerful corporate sponsors on branding, programs, and fundraising campaigns. Earlier in this book, we looked at Feeding America, the nation's leading hunger relief nonprofit, and its branding campaign with SuperValu and the Dairy Council. Indeed, this trend appears to be the basis for acquiring the financial resources, negotiating power, and brand recognition they now enjoy. Just as Sanbonmatsu points to how academic publishers are looking for the most popular and best-selling authors, not necessarily the best work, the commodification of advocacy has created a popularity contest that rewards advocates and organizations on their level of popular appeal to the public. It gives us a great read on what's popular and trending in the short-term, without much concern over the quality of work and long-term impact. The question we should be asking is, to what extent is commodity advocacy in the nonprofit world, and the animal advocates in their sphere of influence, actually advancing animal liberation, considering the current environment in which many of these advocates already embrace this "commodity culture" as the norm?

One manifestation of this trend is the increasing popularity of ranking or rating nonprofits and nonprofit employees based on how well they conform to a corporate philosophy or methodology, as we've seen with effective altruism. Animal Charity Evaluators (ACE) is one such organization that specializes in this kind of analysis of charities. At minimum, any advocate for social justice should consider the ethical implications and shortcomings of evaluating advocacy as we would the performance of a commodity. For example, an organization that ACE might rate as a top charity based on the metric of saving the most animal lives in the present doesn't necessarily mean they are highly influential change makers in the long term. We can probably all agree that gauging the progress of social change over time is far more complex than measuring the performance of a commodity. And most of us can probably see the troubling paradox in using a market-based model of effectiveness that is largely responsible for the gross inequalities and social injustices in the world, rooted in racism, sexism, classism, and, of course, speciesism.

Another manifestation of commodity advocacy is the branding of advocates around a corporate communications model. In such a setting, to be truly effective means playing the game from inside the system and aspiring to the same scripted behavior and psychological tactics used to groom salespeople. In a blog post by Tobias Leenaert, otherwise known as "the Vegan Strategist," Leenaert describes his "You Are Not Your Audience" principle by using a car salesman analogy. He writes, "Like a car salesman, you have to adapt your message to what you think people like, are interested in, are open to, are ready for."[224] Aside from the irony that car salespeople are distrusted and avoided, it's easy to see how this grooming can lead to a kind of shallow conformism, encouraging all facets of the advocate's physical and social presence to be molded around the goal of appealing to what their animal-eating audience would perceive as normal and appealing. We find this methodically presented in Nick Cooney's *Change of Heart* presentation and book in which he explains, "Changing our appearance really will make them more receptive to our message. . . . It took me years to cut my hair and to adopt a more conventional way of dressing."[225] According to this logic, in order to convince someone that a radical change is necessary, we must convince them that we *fit in*. Yes, finding common ground with others is essential, but that doesn't mean we must intentionally mislead them into thinking we agree with them or look and act just like them. On the other hand, the car salesperson wants to sell you a car and will tell you whatever you want to hear to that end.

Even corporate branding and communications experts recognize that deviation from convention can also be just as or more effective. They call it differentiation,[226] or sometimes disruption, a strategy that works a bit like reverse psychology. Differentiation marketing creates surprise, standing out from the crowd or sometimes even creating a new demand for something their audience didn't know they wanted. Differentiation could be said to be an idea that comes from social change. Leaders of social change and political strategy, such as Antonio Gramsci, stress the importance of creating a new social order, a new civilization, where the oppressed overcome oppression and abuse of power, once and for all. The catalyst for this change is what he calls "the modern prince," which "would seek to lead the people out of confusion by teaching them basic literacies for 'seeing,' hence for overcoming power."[227] For Gramsci, it is not about telling people what they want to hear so much as what they need to know to get what they want.

A remarkably successful example of differentiation is Apple's "Think Different" campaign. In the late 1990s, as Apple's reputation and market share had reached rock bottom, Apple launched the "Think Different" campaign, adorning billboards and entire sides of buildings and our TV screens with artistic black-and-white portraits of visionaries like Gandhi, Einstein, the Dalai Lama, and Nelson Mandela. It was a direct appeal to their early adopter base. It was also an appeal to the underdog or the untapped creative potential in all of us. Conventional thinking would have led Apple to run a different kind of campaign, one that appealed to Middle American values. What most people did not realize at the time was that Apple was staging a major comeback with a rebranding campaign that sought to inspire and rally its core base of support from artists and creative professionals. Why? Because Apple knew their base needed a huge morale boost to recover from all the negative media coverage surrounding Apple's fall from grace and to motivate them into becoming Apple's brand champions, who would then transform the Apple brand into mainstream acceptance. Early adopters can do much of the marketing for you (and save you a lot of advertising dollars). This strategy was highly effective for Apple, whose products are now a household name.

One might expect that commodity advocacy borrows the best strategies from corporate branding and marketing, but, instead of cases of highly imaginative and innovative branding like Apple's "Think Different" campaign, we are presented with sleekly-suited-and-tied spokespeople who espouse the tactics of the car salesman. This pop sensibility appeals to people seeking black-and-white answers, cashing in creativity and critical thinking in the name of greater effectiveness. Like pop psychology and self-help, the rhetoric of pop advocacy is more demonstrative, more reductionist, and more prone to faulty logic like false dilemmas and either-or scenarios such as the "do you want to be right or do you want to be effective" example mentioned earlier.

As already discussed, this pop sensibility demands conformity to social and cultural norms as if it were a prerequisite to effective communication. In fact, it would be hard to find advocates of other causes more concerned about what others think or how others perceive them than animal advocates. Why do we care so much? And why are we so fearful of speaking out against the perpetrators of animal injustice? Why do we give them this power to define our identity or how we should best conduct ourselves? Human rights advocates express outrage at the atrocities perpetrated against human victims. And no one ever questions whether this outrage is an appropriate response or call to action. Amnesty International launches entire campaigns around bringing justice to a single human prisoner and exposing the corrupt, unjust system that imprisoned him. Mothers Against Drunk Driving (MADD) understandably conveys anger as the sentiment in the acronym that identifies them, for which they are not faulted for using ineffective messaging. Corporate Accountability International has a popular annual contest called the Corporate Hall of Shame, asking members to vote for the most shameful (unethical) acts of corporate greed and corruption. The focus of attention is not on their behavior as advocates, but rather where it belongs: on the perpetrators and victims of an injustice. Yet advocates for billions of infant and adolescent-age animals are scrutinized for how they conduct themselves, are expected to repress their true feelings and thoughts over an immense injustice and instead present a controlled response, for fear of alienating their audience or for fear of ridicule, criticism, or simply being dismissed as crazy. We give them this power, not only to define us but also to dismiss any serious consideration of the issues we raise. Are we so fearful of negative reactions, of being the messenger who gets shot, that we are willing to repress our valid expression of grief, despair, outrage, and anger over the suffering of animals and instead adopt a composure that enables the very silence and denial we must overcome to advance animal liberation? Packaging advocacy as a commodity presents us with a ludicrous proposition: face animal atrocity and reflect back on society a polished, groomed, sanitized pleasantry.

TRUTH-CENTERED ADVOCACY

The opportunistic approaches and ideas discussed up to now have been justified on the basis of achieving better results or greater effectiveness, and all too often at the expense of truth—that is, at the expense of a clear, consistent, and honest communication platform. Simply put, truth-centered advocacy unleashes the power of truth to combat lies—the lies that keep animals oppressed. We restore to truth a value that protects it from being gambled away for the promise of some other advantage. The fundamental quality of truth strengthens our advocacy, partly because it is so rare and partly because it is essential to winning the trust of our audience, who are far more likely to open their hearts and minds to our message when they recognize that we have no ulterior motive or agenda. Truth is the most pragmatic and effective strategy we have to combat lies, but society won't always readily accept what's true about farmed animals until we first expose what's false, which is the premise of this book. This is because the fictional world of animal agriculture has passed for "truth" for a very long time. It is critical that animal advocates develop the perceptual skills needed to identify these fictions, for their own empowerment and for that of their audience. Like Dorothy pulling back the curtain to expose the feared Oz and discovering that he is just a coward, this process of fiction identification is an essential phase in the disempowerment of animal exploitation. In so doing, we also expose the truth about animal suffering that hides behind this fictional world. To be sure, we will meet resistance in the form of irrelevant distractions, red herrings, and other faulty logical ploys or attempts to discredit the animal rights or vegan position. But with each attempt to distract us away from the real issue, we shift the focus back on where it belongs: the truth about animal exploitation and the culture in which it thrives. Truth-tellers don't need to defend themselves for telling the truth, but liars and institutions built upon lies, and those who defend them, have a lot to answer for.

As we deepen our awareness of the origins and hidden meanings of the words, messages, stories, and visual cues from which these fictions are built, we see how we, other advocates, and society at large have assimilated and used them, albeit inadvertently, in our thoughts, actions, and language. Through truth-centeredness we dismantle archaic vocabularies and rebuild with new ideas, actions, and language from which new stories are born: stories that break through society's learned apathy, denial, and defensiveness, stories that embody the qualities of truth, transparency, and authenticity, featuring *real* people, empathic human caretakers, and incredible animal survivors liberated from the grasp of exploitation.

Truth-centeredness is not necessarily an elaborate or methodical approach to advocacy like those we've discussed earlier. It does not pretend to be a manifesto for a social change movement, but rather a way to ground our actions in sound principles that can complement a wide range of existing forms of activism/advocacy. Truth-centeredness gauges not just effectiveness from the behaviorist model but also things like integrity, clarity, transparency, and creativity—qualities essential to building lasting, trusting, and loyal relationships between both advocates and our audience. It targets, whenever possible, individuals, groups, and institutions that are most sympathetic to our cause. It values repetition as an essential part of our communications strategy necessary to combat a lifetime of repetition from animal-exploitation branding. It values creative expression over conformism, recognizing that the best ideas and actions can only result from an environment that genuinely fosters free thinking and the free and honest exchange of ideas. The best ideas for carrying out our work emerge from creative brainstorming, research, testing, and trial and error. And finally, it values the *why*—why this issue matters to us and building a convincing case for why it should matter to others, honoring Simon Sinek's idea that "inspired leaders think from the inside out, focusing on the *why*."[228]

As truth-tellers, when there is a conflict between reality as we see it and the way we are told to present that reality, we defend our truth above all other motivations—the truth or reality of the victim's experience as well as the truth of our own experience as witnesses—and all the more so because our struggle is against an industry built upon lies and equivocation about the animals it victimizes. When we distort or misrepresent the truth in an attempt to make it more palatable or marketable, we use the exploiter's deceptive tactics. We misrepresent the victim's suffering. We undermine our credibility with others. And we betray our authentic selves as witnesses and messengers. In essence, we find ourselves fueling the culture of denial that helps keep things the way they are while stifling change.

Through truth-centeredness we are humbled by the complexity and enormity of the task we face, and the imperfect and often inconclusive nature of our work, which gives us a healthy skepticism of easy solutions or simplistic evaluations of effectiveness that rely on a single quantifiable metric, corporate standard, or cherry-picked data to advance a single strategy. Truth-centeredness gives us an expansive, long-term, big-picture perspective, focusing our attention on the end goal of liberating animals from their oppressors, rather than squandering our precious time and resources on short-term or short-sighted victories that offer only marginal improvements in the lives of animals at an exceedingly high cost. On the other hand, we recognize that what we urge others to consider is simply an extension of a belief in harm reduction that they already hold but have not yet applied to farmed animals. Truth-centeredness does not reduce the value of our advocacy to facts and figures, such as how many animals we save in the present, but instead leverages a vast body of wisdom about social change from leading intellectuals and activists and from successful past and contemporary social justice efforts. It also leverages the power of visualization to articulate for ourselves and others the kind of world we want to live in, one in which it is no longer socially or culturally acceptable to exploit animals for our own self-serving gains. Truth-centeredness recognizes that cultivating meaningful social change requires doing the hard work of challenging the belief system behind eating animals, and exploitation as a general matter, using creative ways that engage our audience. This harder work is the necessary preparation for the large-scale behavior change we hope for, since dietary change is not the means to that end, but the end result, the logical and moral expression of society's shift in beliefs about eating animals.

ENDNOTES

Foreword

1. Brian Luke, "Justice, Caring, and Animal Liberation," in *The Feminist Care Tradition in Animal Ethics*, ed. Josephine Donovan and Carol J. Adams (New York: Columbia University Press, 2007), 138.
2. Brian Luke, "Taming Ourselves or Going Feral? Toward a Nonpatriarchal Metaethic for Animal Liberation," in *Animals and Women: Feminist Theoretical Explorations*, ed. Carol J. Adams and Josephine Donovan (Durham: Duke University Press, 1995), 314.
3. Tillie Olsen, *Yonnondio: From the Thirties* (New York: Dell, 1974) 135.
4. Josephine Donovan, "Animal Rights and Feminist Theory," in *The Feminist Care Tradition in Animal Ethics*, ed. Josephine Donovan and Carol J. Adams (New York: Columbia University Press, 2007) 76.
5. Stephen Messenger, "Goose Finds Cop and Leads Him to Her Trapped Baby," The Dodo, May 10, 2016, https://www.thedodo.com/goose-leads-cop-trapped-baby-1789420060.html.

Chapters

1. *The Matrix*, directed by Lana and Lilly Wachowski (1999; Burbank, CA: Warner Home Video, 1999), DVD.
2. Melanie Joy, *Why We Love Dogs, Eat Pigs and Wear Cows: An Introduction to Carnism* (Newburyport: Conari Press, 2011), 134.
3. Alan Bullock & Stephen Trombley, eds., *The New Fontana Dictionary of Modern Thought Third Edition* (New York: Harper Collins, 1999), 387–88.
4. "Paradise Camp," *Wikipedia*, last modified July 5, 2015, accessed September 12, 2015, https://en.wikipedia.org/wiki/Paradise_Camp.
5. Harish, "Meat Industry Advertising," Counting Animals, May 7, 2012, http://www.countinganimals.com/meat-industry-advertising/.
6. U.S. Department of Agriculture, *FY 2013 Budget Summary and Annual Performance Plan* (Washington, DC, 2013), 84, http://www.obpa.usda.gov/budsum/FY13budsum.pdf.
7. Ibid.
8. Ibid.
9. Viva, *Viva! Investigates: The Happy Egg Company*, Vimeo video, 6:33, posted by "Viva!," July 9, 2015, https://vimeo.com/133049230.
10. "Study Suggests Chickens Are Smarter Than Toddlers," World Poultry, last modified March 9, 2016, accessed April 11, 2016, http://www.worldpoultry.net/Meat/Articles/2013/6/Study-suggest-chickens-are-smarter-than-toddlers-1289715W/.
11. Philip Low, edited by Jaak Panksepp, Diana Reiss, David Edelman, Bruno Van Swinderen, Philip Low and Christof Koch, "The Cambridge Declaration on Consciousness" (paper presented at the Francis Crick Memorial Conference on Consciousness in Human and non-Human Animals, Cambridge, UK, July 7, 2012).
12. Ibid.
13. Inbal Ben-Ami Bartal, Jean Decety, Peggy Mason, "Empathy and Pro-Social Behavior in Rats," *Science* 334, no. 6061 (December 9, 2011): 1427–1430.
14. Maia Szalavitz, "Rats Show Empathy and Free Their Trapped Companions," *Time*, December 8, 2011, http://healthland.time.com/2011/12/08/rats-show-empathy-and-free-their-trapped-companions/

15. Ibid.
16. "Fish Feel," Fish Feel, accessed May 11, 2016, http://fishfeel.org/PDFs/overview.pdf.
17. "Fish Count Estimates," Fishcount.org.uk, accessed May 11, 2016, http://fishcount. org.uk/fish-count-estimates.
18. R.W.D. Davies et al., "Defining and estimating global marine fisheries bycatch," *Marine Policy* 33, no. 4 (July 2009): 661–672, http://assets.panda.org/downloads/bycatch_paper.pdf.
19. Mary Finelli and Robert Grillo, "Fish Exploited for Food Suffer Like Mammals and Birds," Free From Harm, March 3, 2014, http://freefromharm.org/fish-exploited-for-food-suffer-like-mammals-and-birds/.
20. Culum Brown, "Animal minds: Not just a pretty face," *New Scientist,* June 12, 2004, https://www.newscientist.com/article/mg18224515-200-animal-minds-not-just-a-pretty-face/.
21. Ibid., 2.
22. "Report: Investigation of the killing of tuna in Italy," Animal Equality, accessed May 11, 2016, http://thekillingoftuna.org/report-killing-of-tuna.php
23. "Wild Salmon Direct Operations 2006," YouTube video, 6:07, posted by "wildsalmondirect," November 28, 2006, https://www.youtube.com/watch?v=FzL9ufPvqyg
24. Imperial College London, "Bird brain? Birds and humans have similar brain wiring," *Science Daily,* July 17, 2013, http://www.sciencedaily.com/releases/2013/07/130717095336.htm.
25. Free From Harm Staff Writers, "17 Chicken Facts the Industry Doesn't Want You to Know," Free From Harm, August 28, 2014, http://freefromharm.org/animalagriculture/chicken-facts-industry-doesnt-want-know/.
26. Annie Potts, *Chicken* (London: Reaktion Books, 2012), 34.
27. Robert Grillo, "Chicken Behavior: An Overview of Recent Science," Free From Harm, February 7, 2014, http://freefromharm.org/chicken-behavior-an-overview-of-recent-science/.
28. Rosa Rugani, Lucia Regolin, and Giorgio Vallortigara, "Imprinted numbers: newborn chicks' sensitivity to number vs. continuous extent of objects they have been reared with," *Developmental Science* 13, no. 5 (September 2010): 790–797.
29. "Interview with Chicken Ethologist Dr. Giorgio Vallortigara, University of Trento, Italy," by A Question of Balance, excerpted on *Uncooped,* accessed July 29, 2016, http://www.uncooped.org/.
30. Bob Comis, "Birth, Death, and Money On a Livestock Farm," *HuffPostGreen,* April 21, 2014, http://www.huffingtonpost.com/bob-comis/birth-death-and-money-on-_b_5186257.html.
31. Robert Grillo, "Sanctuaries Teach Us What Farms Can't," Free From Harm, August 29, 2013, http://freefromharm.org/animal-rescue-stories/sanctuaries-teach-us-what-farms-cant/.
32. Marc Bekoff, "Animal Emotions: Exploring Passionate Natures," *BioScience 50, no. 10* (October 2000): 867.
33. Marc Bekoff, "Animal Consciousness and Science Matter," *Psychology Today,* May 7, 2012, http://www.psychologytoday.com/blog/animal-emotions/201205/animal-consciousness-and-science-matter.
34. Marc Bekoff, "Anthropomorphic Double-Talk: Can Animals Be Happy But Not Unhappy? No!" *Psychology Today,* June 24, 2009, https://www.psychologytoday.com/blog/animal-emotions/200906/anthropomorphic-double-talk-can-animals-be-happy-not-unhappy-no.

35. Karen Davis, "The Chicken Anthropomorphized as 'World Conqueror,'" review of *Why Did the Chicken Cross the World? The Epic Saga of the Bird that Powers Civilization,* by Andrew Lawler, *United Poultry Concerns,* December 29, 2014, http://www.upc-online.org/bookreviews/141229_why_did_the_chicken_cross_the_world_review.html.

36. Karen Davis, "Chicken-Human Relationships: from Procrustean Genocide to Empathic Anthropomorphism," in "Minding the Animal Psyche," special issue, *Spring* 83 (Spring 2010), excerpted on United Poultry Concerns, accessed 8/17/15, http://www.upc-online.org/thinking/chicken_human_relationships.pdf.

37. Shree Gopal Goshala, "Importance of Cow and Her Protection," accessed 2/10/16, http://shreegopalgoshala.com/cow-protection/.

38. Will Tuttle, *World Peace Diet* (New York: Lantern Books, 2005), 110.

39. Sherry Colb, *Mind If I Order the Cheeseburger?: And Other Questions People Ask Vegans* (New York: Lantern Books, 2013), 139.

40. Ibid.

41. Tom Regan, *The Case for Animal Rights,* (Berkeley: University of California Press, 1985).

42. Free From Harm Staff Writers, "Animal Law 101: What is 'Necessary' Animal Suffering?," Free From Harm, May 20, 2014, http://freefromharm.org/animals-and-the-law/lesli-bisgoulds-ted-talk-animal-law-101/.

43. "Don't Eat Anything With a Face," Intelligence Squared Debates transcript and video, 1:44:05, from a live debate recorded December 4, 2013, http://intelligencesquaredus.org/debates/past-debates/item/910-dont-eat-anything-with-a-face.

44. Jeffrey Masson, *Beasts: What Animals Can Teach Us About the Origins of Good and Evil* (New York: Bloomsbury, 2015), 66

45. Charles Horn, *Meat Logic: Why Do We Eat Animals?* (North Charleston, SC: CreateSpace, 2014), 84.

46. Colb, *Mind If I Order the Cheeseburger?,*102.

47. Ibid.

48. "Don't Eat Anything With a Face," Intelligence Squared Debates transcript and video.

49. Michael Pollan, "The Intelligent Plant,"*New Yorker,* December 23, http://www.newyorker.com/magazine/2013/12/23/the-intelligent-plant.

50. Adam Merberg, "Should communication between pea plants raise tough issues for vegetarians?" *Say what, Michael Pollan?* (blog), May 1, 2012, https://saywhatmichaelpollan.wordpress.com/2012/05/01/should-communication-between-pea-plants-raise-tough-issues-for-vegetarians/?blogsub=confirming#blog_subscription-3.

51. Barbara Kingsolver, Steven L. Hopp, and Camille Kingsolver, *Animal, Vegetable, Miracle: A Year of Food Life* (New York: HarperTorch, 2007), 224.

52. Jim Mason, *An Unnatural Order* (New York: Lantern Books, 2004), 12.

53. Sherry Colb, "A Response to the Claim That Eating Animals is Natural," Free From Harm, July 25, 2013, http://freefromharm.org/common-justifications-for-eating-animals/its-natural/.

54. Peter H. Kahn and Stephen R. Kellert, eds., *Children and Nature: Psychological, Sociocultural, and Evolutionary Investigations* (Cambridge, MA: MIT Press, 2002).

55. Jeffrey Moussaieff Masson, "Beasts: What animals can teach us about the origins of good and evil," YouTube video, 1:51, posted by "Jeffrey Masson," December 10, 2013, https://www.youtube.com/watch?v=7cUy9u5DdX4.

56. Richard Oppenlander, *Food Choice and Sustainability: Why Buying Local, Eating Less Meat, and Taking Baby Steps Won't Work* (Minneapolis: Langdon Street Press, 2013), 302–303.

57. "The Facts," Cowspiracy, accessed January 22, 2016, http://www.cowspiracy.com/facts/.

58. "AMI Fact Sheet: U.S. Meat and Poultry Production & Consumption: An Overview," American Meat Institute, July 2010, https://www.meatinstitute.org/index.php?ht=a/ GetDocumentAction/i/63785.

59. Gustavo M. Schuenemann, et. al., "A.I. Cover Sheaths Improved Fertility in Lactating Dairy Cows," Progressive Dairyman, October 31, 2011, http://www.progressivedairy. com/topics/a-i-breeding/ai-cover-sheaths-improved-fertility-in-lactating-dairy-cows.

60. DT Lyons, AE Freeman, and AL Kuck, "Genetics of Health Traits in Holstein Cattle," *Journal of Dairy Science* 74, no. 3 (March 1991): 1092–100.

61. "The Welfare of Cows in the Dairy Industry," Humane Society of the United States, accessed July 21, 2014, http://www.humanesociety.org/assets/pdfs/farm/hsus-the-welfare-of-cows-in-the-dairy-industry.pdf.

62. Ibid., 7.

63. "Livestock Slaughter 2013 Summary," USDA National Agricultural Statistics Service, accessed July 21, 2014, http://usda.mannlib.cornell.edu/usda/nass/LiveSlauSu//2010s/2014/ LiveSlauSu-04-21-2014.pdf.

64. "The Welfare of Animals in the Veal Industry," Humane Society of the United States, accessed November 30, 2014, http://www.humanesociety.org/assets/pdfs/farm/hsus-the-welfare-of-animals-in-the-veal-industry.pdf, 7.

65. Ibid.

66. "Health Concerns About Dairy Products," Physicians Committee for Responsible Medicine, accessed November 2, 2014, http://www.pcrm.org/health/diets/vegdiets/ health-concerns-about-dairy-products.

67. Drusilla Banks and Ron Wolford, "Turkey for the Holidays: Turkey Facts," University of Illinois Extension, accessed November 10, 2015, http://urbanext.illinois.edu/turkey/ turkey_facts.cfm.

68. Jennifer Viegas, "Native Americans First Tamed Turkeys 2,000 Years Ago," Discovery News, February 1, 2010, http://news.discovery.com/history/us-history/native-americans -turkeys-domestication.htm.

69. Banks and Wolford, "Turkey for the Holidays: Turkey Facts."

70. Jacob Bunge and David Kesmodel, "America's Move to Soy Hobbles Dairy," *Wall Street Journal*, July 18, 2014, http://www.wsj.com/articles/americas-move-to-soy-hobbles-dairy-1405729869.

71. "Don't be Fooled by the Imitators," YouTube video, 0:22. posted by "REALSEALDairy," April 10, 2014 https://www.youtube.com/watch?v=kS5nXII51Uw&feature=youtu.be.

72. WJ Craig, AR Mangels, and American Dietetic Association, "Position of the American Dietetic Association: vegetarian diets," *Journal of American Dietetic Association*, 109, no. 7 (July 2009), PubMed (19562864).

73. "Hunger Statistics," World Food Programme, accessed December 7, 2015, https:// www.wfp.org/hunger/stats.

74. Tom Knutson, "The killing agency: Wildlife Services' brutal methods leave a trail of animal death," *Sacramento Bee*, April 28, 2012, http://www.sacbee.com/news/investigations/ wildlife-investigation/article2574599.html.

75. "Heifer International," *Wikipedia*, last modified Feburary 27, 2016, accessed December 6, 2015, https://en.wikipedia.org/wiki/Heifer_International.

76. Alton Brown, "Alton Brown Explains How Heifer Passes on the Gift," YouTube video, 2:19, posted by "HeiferInternational," March 22, 2012, https://www.youtube.com/ watch?v=fDIedFMSN64.

77. Dawn Moncrief, "10 Reasons to Say NO To Animal Gifting Hunger Relief Organizations," Free From Harm, December 10, 2013, http://freefromharm.org/ agriculture-environment/10-reasons-to-say-no-to-animal-gifting-hunger-orgs/.

78. Ibid.
79. Joel Marks, "A is for Animal: The Animal User's Lexicon," *Between the Species* 18, no. 1 (August 2015): 2, http://digitalcommons.calpoly.edu/bts/vol18/iss1/1/.
80. Ibid., 7.
81. Joan Dunayer, *Animal Equality: Language and Liberation* (New York: Lantern Books, 2001).
82. Mason, *An Unnatural Order*, 145.
83. Will Tuttle, "What are the Roots of Freedom and Slavery?," One Green Planet, February 23, 2013, http://www.onegreenplanet.org/animalsandnature/what-are-the-roots-of-freedom-and-slavery/.
84. Mason, *An Unnatural Order*, 145.
85. "Artificial Insemination in Goats," YouTube video, 8:46, posted by "Terry Gipson," July 3, 2012, https://www.youtube.com/watch?v=vF89Ar83M7g.
86. "What Are Heritage Breeds?," *The Livestock Conservancy*, accessed December 10, 2015, http://www.livestockconservancy.org/index.php/heritage.
87. Ibid.
88. Ibid.
89. Ibid.
90. Will Anderson, *This Is Hope: Green Vegans and the New Human Ecology* (Lanham, PA: Earth Books, 2013), 150–151.
91. Ibid., 151.
92. Carol J. Adams, *The Sexual Politics of Meat* (New York: Continuum Publishing Company, 2004), 43–44.
93. *Merriam-Webster Online,* s.v. "euthanasia," accessed September, 2015, http://www.merriam-webster.com/dictionary/euthanasia.
94. Hope Bohanec, "Factory Farming vs. Alternative Farming: The Humane Hoax," Free From Harm, March 6, 2014, http://freefromharm.org/animal-products-and-ethics/factory-farming-alternative-farming/.
95. "American Humane Certified Program," Foster Farms, accessed November 10, 2015, http://www.fosterfarms.com/about/ahc.asp.
96. Ibid.
97. Ken White, "A Chicken Leaping Into Every Pot," *HuffPost San Francisco* (blog), May 30, 2013, http://www.huffingtonpost.com/ken-white/a-chicken-leaping-into-ev_b_3355699.html.
98. Mercy for Animals. "What does that 'American Humane Certified' label on your chicken really mean?," accessed February 10, 2016, http://www.americanhumanescam.com
99. Robert Grillo, "The Happy Chicken Farmer Fantasy," Free From Harm, August 19, 2013, http://freefromharm.org/animal-products-and-culture/the-happy-chicken-farmer-fantasy/.
100. Temple Grandin, "How to Determine Insensibility (Unconsciousness) in Cattle, Pigs, and Sheep in Slaughter Plants," Dr. Temple Grandin's Web Page, revised November 2015, accessed July 15, 2015, http://www.grandin.com/humane/insensibility.html.
101. "Temple Grandin on Autism, Death, Celibacy and Cows," by Andrew Goldman, *New York Times Magazine*, April 12, 2013, http://www.nytimes.com/2013/04/14/magazine/temple-grandin-on-autism-death-celibacy-and-cows.html.
102. Grandin, "How to Determine Insensibility (Unconsciousness)."
103. National Turkey Federation, "Turkey Farm & Processing Plant: Temple Grandin," YouTube video, 13:21, posted by "NatlTurkeyFederation," October 8, 2013, http://www.youtube.com/watch?v=852zxDEAR-Q&feature=youtu.be.
104. "If Meat Plants Had Glass Walls," American Meat Institute, accessed July 20, 2015, http://www.animalhandling.org/ht/a/GetDocumentAction/i/89462.

105. Temple Grandin and American Meat Institute Animal Welfare Committee, "Recommended Animal Handling Guidelines & Audit Guide: A Systematic Approach to Animal Welfare," American Meat Institute Foundation, July 2013, rev. 1, http://animalhandling.org/ht/a/GetDocumentAction/i/93003.

106. Karen Davis, Ph.D., "Time to Spread the Joy," Free From Harm, September 17, 2015, http://freefromharm.org/farm-animal-welfare/birds.

107. Ashley Capps, "A Closer Look at What So-Called Humane Farming Means," Free From Harm, September 27, http://freefromharm.org/animal-products-and-ethics/a-comprehensive-analysis-of-the-humane-farming-myth/.

108. Hope Bohanec, *The Ultimate Betrayal: Is There Happy Meat?* (Bloomington, IN: iUniverse, 2013), 14.

109. Sherry F. Colb, "Milk of the Poisonous Tree," *Dorf on Law* (blog), January 7, 2015, http://www.dorfonlaw.org/2015/01/milk-of-poisonous-tree.html.

110. Robert Grillo and Charles Horn, "Backyard Chickens: Expanding our Understanding of 'Harm,'" Free From Harm, May 11, 2014, http://freefromharm.org/farm-animal-welfare/backyard-chickens-expanding-understanding-harm/.

111. Ibid.

112. Hope Bohanec, as quoted in Robert Grillo and Charles Horn, "Backyard Chickens: Expanding our Understanding of 'Harm,'" Free From Harm, May 11, 2014, http://freefromharm.org/farm-animal-welfare/backyard-chickens-expanding-understanding-harm/.

113. Grillo and Horn, "Backyard Chickens."

114. Melanie Joy, "Why We Love Dogs, Eat Pigs, and Wear Cows: An Introduction to Carnism," YouTube video, 1:00:43, filmed February 29, 2012, https://www.youtube.com/watch?v=ZCojVjwJP7o

115. "Sexual Politics of Meat: The Book," CarolJAdams.com, accessed June 2, 2016, http://caroljadams.com/spom-the-book/.

116. C. Daniel Batson et al., "Empathy and Attitudes: Can Feeling for a Member of a Stigmatized Group Improve Feelings Toward the Group?," *Journal of Personality and Social Psychology* 72, no. 1 (1997): 105–118, http://citeseerx.ist.psu.edu/viewdoc/download?doi=10.1.1.495.897&rep=rep1&type=pdf.

117. Sune Borkfelt, Sara Kondrup, Helena Röcklinsberg, Kristian Bjørkdahl, Mickey Gjerris, "Closer to Nature? A Critical Discussion of the Marketing of 'Ethical' Animal Products," *Journal of Agricultural and Environmental Ethics* 28, no. 3 (2015), 21.

118. Ibid., 20

119. Ibid., 19

120. Deborah A. Small, George Loewenstein, and Paul Slovic, "Sympathy and callousness: The impact of deliberative thought on donations to identifiable and statistical victims," *Organizational Behavior and Human Decision Processes* 102, no. 2 (March 2007): 143–153, http://www.sciencedirect.com/science/article/pii/S0749597806000057.

121. "Playboy Interview: Anthony Bourdain," by David Sheff, *Playboy*, October 13, 2011, http://www.playboy.com/articles/anthony-bourdain-interview.

122. "Why Vegetarian?," Kagyu Samye Ling, accessed August 4, 2015, http://www.samyeling.org/about/buddhism-and-meditation/teaching-archive-2/khenpo-tsultrim-lodro/why-vegetarian/.

123. *Merriam-Webster Online*, s.v. "Chicken," accessed April 11, 2016, http://www.merriam-webster.com/dictionary/chicken.

124. Carolynn L. Smith and Jane Johnson, "The Chicken Challenge: What Contemporary Studies Of Fowl Mean For Science And Ethics, Between the Species," *Between the Species* 15, no. 1 (2012): 82, doi:10.15368/bts.2012v15n1.4.

125. Oliver Burkeman, "Believing that life is fair might make you a terrible person," *Guardian*, February 3, 2015, http://www.theguardian.com/commentisfree/oliver-burkeman-column/2015/feb/03/believing-that-life-is-fair-might-make-you-a-terrible-person.

126. Emily Meredith, "My Week on a 'Fact'ory Farm: Part I," Meetingplace, accessed January 10, 2015, http://Meatingplace.com (access now available only to members).

127. Ros Krasny, and Reuters, "Virus Found In Iowa Hog Population, Possibly Beyond," *Chicago Tribune*, May 17 2013, http://articles.chicagotribune.com/2013-05-17/news/sns-rt-us-usda-hogs-virusbre94g0vq-20130517_1_u-s-pork-producers-virus-national-pork-board.

128. Ruth Reichl, "Michael Pollan and Ruth Reichl Hash Out the Food Revolution," *Smithsonian*, June, 2013, http://www.smithsonianmag.com/innovation/michael-pollan-and-ruth-reichl-hash-out-the-food-revolution-74218531/?no-ist=.

129. Mason, *An Unnatural Order*, 190–121.

130. Sasha Boojor, e-mail message to author, September 20, 2015.

131. "Animal Rights," Animal Agriculture Alliance, accessed April 8, 2016, http://www.animalagalliance.org/protect/#animalrights.

132. Ibid.

133. "About Chicken Justice," Chicken Justice, accessed June 4, 2015, http://chickenjustice.org/sample-page/about-chicken-justice/.

134. Ibid.

135. Yadidya Greenberg, "Why I Stand By Urban Adamah," *Forward* (blog), May 8, 2014, April 11, 2016, http://forward.com/food/197846/why-i-stand-by-urban-adamah/.

136. Bohanec, "Factory Farming vs. Alternative Farming."

137. Marnie Hanel, "The Proper Way to Eat a Pig," *New York Times Magazine*, April 4, 2013, http://www.nytimes.com/2013/04/07/magazine/the-proper-way-to-eat-a-pig.html?pagewanted=all&_r=0.

138. Robert Goodland and Jeff Anhang, "Livestock and Climate Change," *World Watch*, November/December 2009, http://www.worldwatch.org/files/pdf/Livestock%20and%20Climate%20Change.pdf.

139. "'Free-Range' Poultry and Eggs," United Poultry Concerns, accessed May 13, 2016, http://www.upc-online.org/freerange.html.

140. Free From Harm Staff Writers, "17 Chicken Facts the Industry Doesn't Want You to Know."

141. Ali Berlow, "Blessed Meat," *Ali Berlow* (blog), March 4, 2013, http://www.aliberlow.com/articles/2013/3/4/blessed-meat.

142. Jill Waldbieser, "The Scary Mental Health Risks of Going Meatless," *Women's Health*, December 2, 2015, http://www.womenshealthmag.com/food/side-effects-of-vegetarianism.

143. Rob Dunn, "Human Ancestors Were Nearly All Vegetarians," *Scientific American*, July 23, 2013, http://blogs.scientificamerican.com/guest-blog/human-ancestors-were-nearly-all-vegetarians/.

144. Dan Pine and Andy Altman-Ohr, "Under Pressure, Urban Adamah Cancels Kosher Slaughter Workshop," *j. the Jewish News Weekly of Northern California*, May 1, 2014, http://www.jweekly.com/article/full/71553/under-pressure-urban-adamah-cancels-kosher-slaughter-workshop/.

145. Jerry Adler and Andres Lawler, "How The Chicken Conquered The World," *Smithsonian*, June 2012, http://www.smithsonianmag.com/history/how-the-chicken-conquered-the-world-87583657/.

146. "The Jungle Introduction," synopsis of *The Jungle*, by Upton Sinclair, Shmoop, accessed December 4, 2015, http://www.shmoop.com/the-jungle/.

147. Leah Eisenstadt, "Birds of a Feather Inherit Together," Broad Institute, March 10, 2010, https://www.broadinstitute.org/news/1430.

148. "Modern Meat Chicken Industry," PennState Extension, accessed July 4, 2015, http://extension.psu.edu/animals/poultry/topics/general-educational-material/the-chicken/modern-meat-chicken-industry.

149. Ibid.

150. Matt Ridley, "Reasons to Crow About Ever-Bigger Chickens," *Wall Street Journal*, October 22, 2011, http://www.wsj.com/articles/SB1000142405297020434610457663721068661 3464.

151. Karen Davis, "Eliminating the Suffering of Chickens Bred for Meat," United Poultry Concerns, February 24, 2013, http://www.upc-online.org/broiler/130224eliminating_suffering.html.

152. Olivia Solon, "Food Project Proposes Matrix-Style Vertical Chicken Farms," *Wired*, February 15, 2012, http://www.wired.com/2012/02/headless-chicken-solution/.

153. Mark Cartwright, "Slavery in the Roman World," *Ancient History Encyclopedia*, November 1, 2013, http://www.ancient.eu/article/629/.

154. "Not as bad as," *RationalWiki*, last modified March 11, 2016, accessed November 28, 2015, http://rationalwiki.org/wiki/Not_as_bad_as.

155. Horn, *Meat Logic*, 82.

156. Sylvain Bonhommeau, Laurent Dubroca, Olivier Le Pape, Julien Barde, David M. Kaplan, Emmanuel Chassot, and Anne-Elise Nieblas, "Eating up the world's food web and the human trophic level," *PNAS* 110, no. 51 (December 17, 2013), http://www.pnas.org/content/110/51/20617

157. Ibid.

158. Ana Navarrete, Carel P. van Schaik and Karin Isler, "Energetics and the evolution of human brain size," *Nature* 480 (December 1, 2011): 91–91, http://www.nature.com/nature/journal/v480/n7375/full/nature10629.html.

159. Lesley J. Rogers, *The Development of Brain and Behaviour in the Chicken* (Wallingford, UK: CAB International, 1995), 231.

160. Lauri Harvey Keagle, "Fair Oaks Officially Kicks Off New Pig Adventure," *Northwest Indiana Times*, August 5, 2013, http://www.nwitimes.com/business/local/fair-oaks-officially-kicks-off-new-pig-adventure/article_85d55ea9-262a-5790-930b-481b15729c8a.html.

161. Peter Gould, "Problem Dog," *Breaking Bad*, season 4, episode 7, aired August 28, 2011, accessed April 11, 2016 on Netflix.

162. Jodie Foster, "Comic Sans," *Orange is the New Black*, season 2, episode 7, directed by Andrew McCarthy, aired June 6, 2014, accessed April 11, 2016 on Netflix.

163. "How to Do Animal Rights: Chicken Statistics," How To Do Animal Rights, accessed 7/21/2014, http://animalethics.org.uk/i-ch7-2-chickens.html.

164. "The Welfare of Animals in the Egg Industry," Humane Society of the United States, accessed 7/21/2014, http://www.humanesociety.org/assets/pdfs/farm/welfare_egg.pdf.

165. To give you an idea of how unnatural domestic egg production is, consider the habits of the wild jungle fowl: "Unlike most domestic hens, who have been selectively bred to lay eggs year-round, wild fowl breed and lay primarily in spring. The Red Jungle Fowl lays 10-15 eggs per year, and the average size of each brood is 4-6 chicks." "About Chickens," Humane Society of the United States, accessed 2/11/2014, http://www.humanesociety.org/assets/pdfs/farm/about_chickens.pdf.

166. Ashley Capps, "Catching Up With Science: Burying the 'Humans Need Meat' Argument," Free From Harm, July 17, 2013, http://freefromharm.org/health-nutrition/catching-up-with-science-burying-the-humans-need-meat-argument/.

167. Paul Rozin, Julia M. Hormes, Myles S. Faith and Brian Wansink, "Is Meat Male? A Quantitative Multimethod Framework to Establish Metaphoric Relationships," *Journal of Consumer Research* 39, no. 3 (October 2012): 629–643, doi:10.1086/664970.

168. Free From Harm Staff Writers, "The Power of Images in Shaping Popular Culture," Free From Harm, March 2, 2013, http://freefromharm.org/animal-products-and-culture/the-power-of-images-in-shaping-popular-culture/.

169. US Department of Agriculture and National Agricultural Statistics Service, "2007 Census of Agriculture: Women Farmers," p. 1, accessed January, 10, 2016, http://www.agcensus.usda.gov/Publications/2007/Online_Highlights/Fact_Sheets/Demographics/women.pdf

170. Carmen M. Cusack, "Feminism and Husbandry: Drawing the Fine Line Between Mine and Bovine," *Journal of Critical Animal Studies* 11, no. 1 (2013): 24–45, http://www.criticalanimalstudies.org/volume-11-issue-1-2013/.

171. Victoria Johnson, "Everyday Practices of the Master Race: Fascist Stratification and the Fluidity of 'Animal' Domination," in *Critical Theory and Animal Liberation*, ed. John Sambonmatsu (Lanham, MD: Rowman & Littlefield Publishers, 2011), 212.

172. S.L. Davis, "The Least Harm Principle May Require That Humans Consume a Diet Containing Large Herbivores, Not a Vegan Diet," *Journal of Agricultural and Environmental Ethics* 16, no. 4 (July 2003): 387–394.

173. Kate Murphy, "Blessed Be My Freshly Slaughtered Dinner," *New York Times*, September 5, 2015, http://www.nytimes.com/2015/09/06/sunday-review/blessed-be-my-freshly-slaughtered-dinner.html.

174. Ibid.

175. Mark Middleton, "Number of Animals Killed to Produce One Million Calories in Eight Food Categories," AnimalVisuals, October 12, 2009, http://www.animalvisuals.org/projects/data/1mc/.

176. Gary L. Francione, "There Is No Third Choice," *Animal Rights: The Abolitionist Approach* (blog), December 4, 2015, http://www.abolitionistapproach.com/there-is-no-third-choice/#.Vwf2MRMrI1h.

177. Gary L. Francione, "Adventures in Missing the Point and Confused Thinking," Gary L. Francione: The Abolitionist Approach to Animal Rights Facebook page, accessed April 11, 2016, https://www.facebook.com/abolitionistapproach/posts/591193867567038.

178. "About Us," Fair Oaks Farms, accessed August 1, 2013, http://fofarms.com/about-us.

179. Ashley Capps, "Pig Adventure Virtual Tour: The First Factory Farm Disneyland," Free From Harm, August 20, 2013, http://freefromharm.org/animal-cruelty-investigation/pig-adventure-virtual-tour-the-first-factory-farm-disneyland/.

180. 4-H, accessed April 8, 2016, http://www.4-h.org/.

181. Colter Ellis and Leslie Irvine, "Reproducing Dominion: Emotional Apprenticeship in the 4H Youth Livestock Program," *Society and Animals* 18, no. 1 (2010):21–39, Brill Online (doi: 10.1163/106311110X12586086158402).

182. Kate Stewart and Matthew Cole, "The Conceptual Separation of Food and Animals in Childhood," *Food, Culture & Society: An International Journal of Multidisciplinary Research* 12, no. 4 (2009): 457–476, doi:10.2752/175174409X456746.

183. Ibid., 466.

184. Ibid., 465. .

185. Ibid., 468.

186. Steve Savage, "No, Cows Don't Make Fertilizer," *Applied Mythology* (blog), March 18, 2013, http://appliedmythology.blogspot.com/2013/03/no-cows-dont-make-fertilizer.html.

187. Ibid.

188. "Haber process," *Wikipedia*, last modified April 28, 2016, accessed January 23, 2016, https://en.wikipedia.org/wiki/Haber_process.

189. Robin McKie, "From fertiliser to Zyklon B: 100 years of the scientific discovery that brought life and death," *Guardian*, November 2, 2013, https://www.theguardian.com/science/2013/nov/03/fritz-haber-fertiliser-ammonia-centenary.

190. Brie Mazurek, "A More Humane Way to Breed Laying Hens," Civil Eats, August 11, 2014, http://civileats.com/2014/08/11/this-farmer-has-found-a-humane-way-to-breed-laying-hens/.

191. Potts, *Chicken*, 9.

192. Mazurek, "A More Humane Way to Breed Laying Hens."

193. Ibid.

194. Ibid.

195. "About Chickens," Humane Society of the United States, accessed August 21, 2015, http://www.humanesociety.org/assets/pdfs/farm/about_chickens.pdf.

196. Will Anderson, e-mail message to author, August 10, 2014, commenting on http://www.cuesa.org/seller/eatwell-farm.

197. Ibid.

198. David Crary, "Pigs Smart as Dogs? Activists Pose the Question," *CNSNews.com*, July 29, 2013, http://www.cnsnews.com/news/article/pigs-smart-dogs-activists-pose-question.

199. Melanie Joy, "Speaking Truth to Power: Understanding the Dominant, Animal-Eating Narrative for Vegan Empowerment and Social Transformation," One Green Plant, January 21, 2013, http://www.onegreenplanet.org/animalsandnature/speaking-truth-to-power-understanding-the-dominant-animal-eating-narrative-for-vegan-empowerment-and-social-transformation/.

200. Ibid.

201. Mylan Engel, "The Immorality of Eating Meating," in *The Moral Life: An Introductory Reader in Ethics and Literature*, ed. Louis P. Pojman (New York: Oxford University Press, 2000), 859, http://www.uta.edu/philosophy/faculty/burgess-jackson/Engel,%20The%20Immorality%20of%20Eating%20Meat%20(2000).pdf.

202. "Number of Animals vs. Amount of Donations," Animal Charity Evaluators, accessed January 12, 2016, http://www.animalcharityevaluators.org/research/foundational-research/number-of-animals-vs-amount-of-donations/.

203. Harish, "Meat Industry Advertising."

204. Simon Sinek, "How Great Leaders Inspire Action," TED video, 18:04, filmed September 2009, http://www.ted.com/talks/simon_sinek_how_great_leaders_inspire_action?language=en.

205. "Faunalytics Data Analysis Method: Method Used to Obtain Average Length of Vegetarianism from Faunalytics Data," Animal Charity Evaluators, accessed January 10, 2016, http://www.animalcharityevaluators.org/research/foundational-research/vegetarian-recidivism/hrc-data-analysis-method/.

206. Sinek, "How Great Leaders Inspire Action," TED video.

207. "How Many Former Vegetarians and Vegans Are There?" Faunalytics, accessed January 2, 2016, https://faunalytics.org/how-many-former-vegetarians-and-vegans-are-there/.

208. Nick Cooney, "Change Of Heart: What Psychology Can Teach Us About Spreading Social Change," Vimeo video, 44:36, posted by "The Humane League," February 27, 2011, https://vimeo.com/20456520.

209. Tanya Chartrand, Shannon Pinckert, and Jerry M. Burger, (1999). "When Manipulation Backfires: The Effects of Time Delay and Requester on the Foot-in-the-Door Technique," *Journal of Applied Social Psychology* 29, no. 1 (1999): 212, https://faculty.fuqua.duke.edu/~tlc10/bio/TLC_articles/1999/Chartrand_Pinckert_Burger_1999.pdf.

210. Carol A. Scott, "Modifying Socially-Conscious Behavior: The Foot-in-the-door Technique," *Journal of Consumer Research* 4, no. 3 (1977): 156–64, http://www.jstor.org/stable/2488643.

211. James P. Dillard, "The Current Status of Research on Sequential-Request Compliance Techniques," *Personality and Social Psychology Bulletin* 17, no. 3 (June 1991): 283-288, doi: 10.1177/0146167291173008.

212. "Consumer Perceptions of Farm Animal Welfare," Animal Welfare Institute, accessed January 10, 2016, https://awionline.org/sites/default/files/uploads/documents/fa-consumer_perceptionsoffarmwelfare_-112511.pdf.

213. Brian Kateman, "Ending the Battle Between Vegans, Vegetarians, and Everyone Else," TEDx video, 18:07, filmed in New York, November 2014, posted Dec. 19, 2014, http://tedxtalks.ted.com/video/Ending-the-battle-between-vegan;TEDxCUNY.

214. "What We Do," Humane League Labs, accessed January 3, 2016, https://humaneleaguelabs.wordpress.com/what-we-do/.

215. Ibid.

216. "Meat Substitutes Market by Type (tofu & tofu ingredients, tempeh, TVP, quorn, other soy products, seitan, & others), Source (soy-based, wheat-based, mycoprotein, & others), Category (frozen & refrigerated), & by Region - Global Forecast to 2020," Markets and Markets, August 2015, http://www.marketsandmarkets.com/Market-Reports/meat-substitutes-market-979.html.

217. Many people don't count dairy and eggs and don't look at how many of the processed or packaged foods they consume contain animal ingredients.

218. "Report: Which Request Creates The Most Diet Change, 'Vegan,' 'Vegetarian, 'Eat Less Meat,' or 'Cut Out or Cut Back On,' Animal Products?" Humane League Labs, September 20, 2015, https://humaneleaguelabs.wordpress.com/2015/09/20/report-which-request-creates-the-most-diet-change-vegan-vegetarian-eat-less-meat-or-cut-out-or-cut-back-on-animal-products/.

219. Ibid.

220. Casey Taft, "Pseudoscience in the Animal Rights Movement," Vegan Publishers, October 18, 2015, http://veganpublishers.com/pseudoscience/.

221. Carol J. Adams, "The Sexual Politics of Meat and Powerful Political Women," *Carol J. Adams* (blog), June 12, 2013, http://caroljadams.blogspot.com/search?q=Meat%2C+after+all%2C+has+no+power.

222. Ashley Capps, "12 Important Reasons to Go Vegan Today," Free From Harm, February 28, 2014, http://freefromharm.org/why-vegan/.

223. John Sanbonmatsu, *The Postmodern Prince: Critical Theory, Left Strategy, and the Making of a New Political Subject* (New York: Monthly Review Press, 2004), 75–96.

224. Tobias Leenaert, "You Are Not Your Audience," The Vegan Strategist, January 5, 2016, http://veganstrategist.org/2016/01/05/you-are-not-your-audience/.

225. Cooney, "Change Of Heart," Vimeo video.

226. Bethany Shepard, "10 Brands That Brilliantly Differentiated Themselves From the Competition," HubSpot Blogs, June 30, 2014, http://blog.hubspot.com/marketing/branding-differentiate-competition-examples.

227. John Sanbonmatsu, *The Postmodern Prince*, 147.

228. Sinek, "How Great Leaders Inspire Action," TED video.